KICK SOME SaaS

STEWART MARSHALL

First published in 2023 by Stewart Marshall

© Stewart Marshall 2023
The moral rights of the author have been asserted

All inquiries should be made to the author.

A catalogue entry for this book is available from the National Library of Australia.

ISBN: 978-1-922764-94-2

Printed in Australia by McPherson's Printing
Book production and text design by Publish Central
Cover design by Pipeline Design

The paper this book is printed on is certified as environmentally friendly.

Disclaimer: The material in this publication is of the nature of general comment only, and does not represent professional advice. It is not intended to provide specific guidance for particular circumstances and it should not be relied on as the basis for any decision to take action or not take action on any matter which it covers. Readers should obtain professional advice where appropriate, before making any such decision. To the maximum extent permitted by law, the author and publisher disclaim all responsibility and liability to any person, arising directly or indirectly from any person taking or not taking action based on the information in this publication.

CONTENTS

For Denis for helping me change direction.
For Carolyn and Jo for helping me find the right path.
And for Alison without whom I'd be completely lost.

FOREWORD

All day, every day, innumerable software systems guide us through our lives. Yet, as Stewart Marshall asserts in this deep dive into the world of software and innovation, 'If you're looking at the technology, you're missing the point.'

He should know. With over 30 years in the IT industry, and much of that spent in R&D and leadership creating tools and solutions for the international market, he's one of Australia's leading authorities on SaaS and commercial software.

In *Kick Some SaaS*, Stewart takes business leaders and software entrepreneurs on a journey from ideation through to commercialisation and beyond. His use of plain English and non-technical language makes the content accessible to all, regardless of their background, and combined with a liberal smattering of his native British understatement and dry wit, what might be a dangerously dull subject matter is instead engaging and entertaining. It's a must read for anyone looking to take their place in the software world.

On the surface, this is a book about creating and selling technology. But behind the cautionary tales, top tips and numerous lists to guide the reader towards success lies another far more important theme. Throughout, Stewart directs our gaze away from the bits, bytes and baffling, instead directing it towards the needs and wants of the myriad people for whom software is an ever-ready servant.

Having had the honour and pleasure of guiding some of the world's biggest enterprises through the technological turmoil of the last forty to fifty years, this is a sentiment that very much rings true for me.

No technology business, from the smallest of start-ups to the largest of multinationals, can afford to ignore its people. As Stewart writes, 'It's man and machine, not man or', and as the fourth industrial revolution continues apace, and we seek new and innovative ways of improving our lives, it is essential that we consider the needs of humanity and our home both today and in the longer term.

There is then perhaps no more important topic than that of sustainability, a subject close to my heart and Stewart's as well. While the wheels of government policy turn slowly, business can act almost immediately, and SaaS organisations are perfectly placed to deliver global impact at scale, whether business to business or consumer.

Kick Some SaaS then is about so much more than software and technology. It's a call to arms. It's an appeal to those creating tomorrow's world today to be equitable, genuine and authentic in all they do. And it's a book about Stewart's vision of a future where purposeful action is the cornerstone of those innumerable software systems that touch our daily lives.

I for one hope he succeeds. Such ideals lie at the heart of a truly sustainable future. And when he does, should we take a moment to gaze upon our technological mastery, the point will be abundantly clear for all to see.

David Thodey AO
Chairperson of Xero and Tyro Payments

CHAPTER 1

ALL THAT'S GONE BEFORE

NOT MUCH HAS HAPPENED ...

That well over half of all humans are connected to each other by the computer in their pocket is quite literally the stuff of my childhood dreams. Not that I ever envisioned the likes of YouTube, Facebook, Instagram, TikTok or any of the myriad services available today, but by the early 1980s computers had already transformed from room-filling behemoths to the personal desktop computer, and the ongoing miniaturisation of technology meant the path ahead was plain to see.

By the time I finished my formal education, powerful personal computers could be bought relatively cheaply, and the age of home and mass-market computing was a foregone conclusion.

And then came 6 August 1991. Now that's what I call a red-letter day.

I was twenty-two years old and just three weeks away from starting my first proper job using my newly learned IT skills. It was a Tuesday and Bryan Adams's *Everything I Do* was number one, again, just about everywhere. I don't remember what I was doing that day, but I was probably enjoying my last few moments of unemployment with a little fishing in the rather idyllic part of rural Warwickshire where I grew up.

And as I was whiling away the hours, Tim Berners-Lee had just created the first ever website and was running it on the first ever browser, WorldWideWeb.

Not much has happened since then though, apart from the rise, rise and continued rise of the internet. We have global connectivity. Hundreds of millions of PCs and laptops are shipped each year. An estimated 14, 15, 16, 17 … billion mobile devices are in use, and just to make sure my opening will seem suitably dated in years to come, the worldwide roll out of 5G is charging ahead, and China has already launched a 6G satellite.

And if that's not enough, literally trillions of IOT (Internet of Things) devices are on the way.

Some 4.1 billion people now have online access, 850 million or so of them in China, and Northern Europe gets the bragging rights with a staggering 95% of people getting online.

And anyone who's doing just that has plenty of stuff to look at on the roughly 1.75 billion websites. If you loaded one website per second, it would take 55-and-a-half years to see them all.

Not as many as you think are dedicated to pornography, and more than you'd hope are in some way related to cats. YouTube alone has millions of feline videos, and they've been viewed billions of times, possibly even trillions. And if it isn't our furry friends, it's some other facet of the human condition with its own dedicated corner of the online world, such is our obsession with the monstrous marvel we've created.

For those born in the Western World since 2000, a life without the internet is almost unfathomable. It's all but ubiquitous, and we feel lost without it. Whether we're tweeting on Twitter, snapping on Snapchat, doing our banking, buying on Amazon, managing small business accounts on Xero, or whatever, our civilisation is now utterly entwined with all that our technological wunderkind, and its almost endless services, has to offer.

And yet the modern internet isn't even thirty. It's a mere babe by technology standards, and we are only just beginning to leverage its power. So, there's going to be a lot more where that came from, and for those prepared to invest in its continued success, there will be some very exciting opportunities ahead.

THE LATEST AND GREATEST WAY OF DELIVERING SOFTWARE

Given that I describe myself as a 'SaaS and commercial software adviser' and 'Translator of IT gibberish', I'll remain true to brand and tell you that this is not a technical book. There's little to nothing in here about the specifics of programming or how to write code, and neither is it a detailed treatise on the finer points of marketing or sales. But, if you or your team are making software, either to sell or to enhance your business operations, you're in precisely the right place.

Whether you know it or not yet, you're probably in the SaaS world as well, and if you ask me, it's one of the most exciting places to be. I'm biased of course, but that doesn't make me wrong.

SaaS (Software as a Service, usually pronounced 'sass') is the latest and greatest way of delivering software, and it usually means we're talking about something that exists somewhere in the cloud being used by lots of people in a browser. But it doesn't have to be like that and there really aren't any rules, so as long as you're creating software solutions for your fellow humans to use, we're going to get along just fine.

Most likely is that you're a business leader and a subject matter expert. You're probably intimately familiar with your market, and the many problems that your prospects, customers and team face daily. But, when it comes to the staggeringly complex and expensive world of software development and ownership, and the almost Herculean task of trying to find people to make it, buy it and use it, you likely find yourself wondering which of the many tasks on your to-do list to prioritise.

Or you may be a technician and have all the programming skills you'll ever need. But while you might save a few bucks on development costs, at some point the world of commerce is going to slap you around and you're going to have to deal with all that business stuff. If you don't, the software you're creating will be nothing more than a rather expensive and time-consuming hobby.

THE DYSTOPIAN RACE TO THE BOTTOM

If you're lucky, your business is already mature enough and rich enough to afford a reasonable-size team. But for most, ongoing software development and marketing costs mean that there are only a few dollars left over. The result is that a small team is left to manage a wide variety of tasks as they try to grow the business, and the boss is left wearing many hats and working long days.

It's easy in this situation to focus attention on the software itself, but with limited experience of the development process, understanding where all the time and money goes – and where it *should* go – is difficult. And you're not helped by a tech team that seems to speak a different language. Development delays are common, as are budget overruns, and you seem to be forever chasing your tail, with prospects and customers demanding new functionality. But no matter how many toys you give them to play with, they rarely seem happy for long.

To cap it all, some of your customers, who just months ago were enthusiastically signing up, are now beginning to drift away. What little feedback you get from them tells you that they're no longer satisfied with the experience, despite your best efforts to appease them. Attrition rates slowly rise, and customer lifetime value begins to decline, impacting your bottom line.

In an effort to reverse the trend, you spread your marketing nets a little wider. Acquisition costs begin to increase, putting a further squeeze on the budget. Almost inevitably, prices are cut as you try to find as many prospects as you can to fill the sales funnel. Lower-grade clients sign up, but as they're not really your target market, their commitment to your platform is low.

For many SaaS businesses, this dystopian race to the bottom is all too familiar. A technology focus, development problems, insatiable prospects and customers continually demanding more for less, and a churn rate that's far too high leave them trying to make more technology to end a cycle that eventually drains the business of resources. Without intervention and additional investment capital, they become just another statistic, one of the over 90% of SaaS businesses that do not survive much more than three years.

Happily, with a few relatively minor adjustments, a vicious cycle can be transformed into a virtuous one. And it starts with me introducing you to my favourite saying:

If you're looking at the technology, you're missing the point.

You don't have to memorise it now. It's going to come up again.

Top SaaS tip: If your platform isn't solving problems, it's creating them.

IF YOU'RE LOOKING AT THE TECHNOLOGY, YOU'RE MISSING THE POINT

Success in SaaS is all about playing the long game, and to do that you need both *software* and *service*, because both Ss are equally valuable. Get that right and you can avoid the costly and nearly always fatal race to the bottom. And that's for the best, because the only winner of that is the business that picks up your customers when you go broke.

Instead of focusing on your platform, look at the people you're serving. Think about how wonderful life would be if they were happy, high-quality customers paying good money for many years. Or perhaps they are a slick, efficient, productive and happy team, because that's what you should be aiming for.

Do you really think a bit of software is the only thing that's important to them?

They're people. They want so much more than that. They want to be loved, to feel they're part of a community, and they probably want to make a difference somehow. After all, we've spent the last couple of decades or so teaching our younger generations they need to look after the planet and each other, so get that right and you have a far greater chance of success.

Start with your people: those you *really want* as customers and colleagues. If you engage with the wrong people, it's a cost to your business. The time, money and effort you spent chasing and managing them would be far more valuable if you were wrangling the right people.

Focus your efforts on them and their needs rather than wants, so that your solution solves their problems. Rather than trying to be all things to all people, your product development can then be so much more precise. You'll have fewer things to make and far less chance of wasting time. Then you can focus squarely on the second S of SaaS, *service*. Rather than them climbing aboard and being left to it, you can lavish your attention upon them, giving them the SaaS equivalent of the five-star treatment with education, support, help and a purpose-led community to engage with.

A TRANSLATOR OF IT GIBBERISH

There are many wonderfully clever people in the IT industry. On my more confident days I like to think I might be included in their number. But despite their abundant intelligence, they do have a disturbing tendency to use abbreviations and technical language and talk in a way that can probably best be described as self-serving mumbo jumbo.

Many specialist groups are the same – like doctors and lawyers. I'm convinced it's a technique they use to try to make themselves sound more interesting and erudite. It also keeps us mere mortals suitably in the dark about what they're up to, which is an odd thing when you think about it. After all, we are the customer and it is us that's going to bear the brunt of the outcomes, be they good or bad.

I, however, am not one for such nonsense … mostly. (We're all human after all.) That is not to say that I can't speak their language. I'm more than capable of taking a bit of a byte out of the technological Apple should the need arise.

See what I did there?

Bit, and byte?

Two delicious technology puns.

Yeah, I know – it's pretty low grade, but look at what I've got to work with. And I don't suppose it'll get much better than that either, so you might as well set your humour expectations to an appropriate level now to avoid disappointment later.

Happily, the information about SaaS and software is top notch, and I'm sure that'll make up for it.

Anyway, the point is that I much prefer to refer to things in terms that the normal person on the street will understand. I find I have far more free-flowing conversations that way, and because I pride myself on my ability to speak in plain English, I like to convey that skill as part of my market positioning. So, I describe myself as a Translator of IT gibberish. I could have gone with 'Speaker of plain English', but that seemed a little boring. And as that's another trait often associated with IT geeks, I thought I'd try something a tiny bit wittier.

If there's one thing that can safely be said about me, it's that I'm definitely not a typical IT guy (mostly).

THE IT INDUSTRY AND ME

And that brings me nicely to my *official* title of 'SaaS and commercial software adviser', a name I came up with having spent two years trying on many others, with none of them quite fitting properly.

I've been in the IT game for thirty years or so and I've done many roles. I've been in executive leadership for an S&P/ASX 50 global vendor, consulted to large enterprises, governments, academia and businesses of all sizes down to the earliest of start-ups. I've been in technical support, presales, development, training, project management and more. Much of my time has been spent inventing, designing, building and trying to sell tools and solutions used by thousands of businesses in Australia and around the world, including the likes of Proctor & Gamble, Kawasaki and Honda. I've specialised in high-speed development tools, and spent twenty years making software to make making more software quicker and cheaper.

If you're confused by the idea of that, you're not alone. Whenever I explained this to people at a Sunday afternoon barbie, there was typically a pause while the notion was digested, then an almost inevitable, 'Umm … oh look, I need to get another drink. Please excuse me.'

Career 1.0

My life in the world of technology certainly wasn't planned. In fact, most of my professional life is adequately summed up when I say that everything I've done seemed like a good idea at the time.

The PC came on the market the year I started high school, so there was little to no formal computer education at the time. And there certainly weren't any classes at the traditional school I attended. In many ways, that had changed little since the 1950s, and it was soon evident that school's classical academic approach and I weren't going to hit it off. So, despite being in the top few percent of the county at an early age and attending the prestigious King Edward VI grammar school in Stratford-upon-Avon, I found myself in a variety of in-between jobs.

After eighteen months of treading water, I decided that learning about computers was probably a good move for the future. I'd always had an interest in technology, and as computers were turning up just about everywhere by the late 1980s, it seemed like a good idea.

I have never looked back.

By 1996 I'd started working in the UK office for LANSA, an internationally recognised Australian vendor of high-speed development tools, and it was here that I began to realise I was completely at home in the software world. I enjoyed programming, but this required so much more. I didn't just write code. I was expected to understand the bigger picture, to question the status quo, to have an opinion and to argue my case. I knew within a few days that commercial software and I were going to get on very well indeed.

I also had a bit of a thing about Australia. Ignoring that they were the arch cricketing and rugby enemy during my formative years, *Crocodile Dundee* and the eternal sunshine of *Neighbours* had already sold the lifestyle to me. On top of that, my maternal grandfather – who'd been a relatively poor tenant farmer his whole life – had a strange fascination with the land Down Under and I think his enthusiasm must have rubbed off on me.

So it was that after working with a few Aussies I was keen to take whatever opportunities were available, and my wife and I were fortunate enough to get a cheap holiday in Sydney in 1999 courtesy of a colleague. It was the run-up to the Olympics and it was a magical time to be there. Everything was clean and shiny. I was hooked.

We went home and I emailed the boss asking if I could work in the Sydney office, and we moved there in 2000. This too seemed a good idea at the time.

LANSA is what used to be called a CASE (computer-aided software engineering) tool. Today this is referred to as 'low code', and there are many vendors in the space. Rather than a programmer writing hundreds of lines, low-code tools do much of it for you. As far as I'm concerned, that's just how it should be. After all, computers are supposed to help us be better at whatever it is we're doing, so software that helps you make more software seems entirely reasonable.

The ideas behind LANSA – reducing complexity and empowering people – have followed me throughout my career. And I still apply them today when working with SaaS vendors, encouraging them to put the needs of their prospects and customers front and centre as they build their tools and supporting environments.

These are ideas that will come up regularly as we go.

Career 2.0

In mid-2017, after twenty years at LANSA and having been the driving force behind its latest and greatest offering, I'd reached the point in my career where it was time to move on, and I was trying to determine a path forward.

A chance meeting at a Sunday afternoon barbecue would change everything.

Enter Denis, a wise old man of the IT industry who happened to live just a few doors away. He'd been the CEO of a large IT business, a consultant, had worked all over the world, and seemed to know everyone. We started chatting and it soon became clear that we shared a great many opinions, and a friendship was born. A few weeks later we were discussing my employment options and how I felt a bit trapped, and he asked me how old I was. I told him forty-eight.

'That's plenty of time for a second career,' was his reply, and at that precise moment a lightbulb turned on, illuminating a hitherto unseen world of opportunity. I didn't know what I was going to do or how, but I suddenly knew that LANSA was no longer the right place for me. By Christmas I'd given up a perfectly decent job and made the leap. I was unemployed for the first time in years. And so, in January 2018, I went out into the big wide world intent on selling my wit and wisdom to whoever needed it most.

I'd started writing about the industry and had discovered I was quite good at it, but I had no idea what to do with this newfound skill and certainly no concept as to how I'd monetise it. A friend suggested

I attend an event about the KPI (Key Person of Influence) program run by Dent Global, and having nothing better to do, I did just that.

I was sold, and signed up a couple of weeks later, and I convinced a friend to join as well. This got me an invitation to a special ambassadors' event, and it was here that my perspective on life changed completely.

Stew 2.0

I'd spent my career as a backroom boy in a software company. In many senses my world had remained unchanged for years. And then I met a room full of entrepreneurs, and they were not only running their own businesses, they were also doing good and making a difference to others' lives. They were giving a small amount of their revenue to help those in need. They were engaging in conscious capitalism, the environment, social purpose and the United Nations' seventeen global goals. And they were showing how you could embed these ideas in business too, and not only did this help make the world a better place, it was good for the bottom line as well.

I knew instantly that I loved every bit of this. I didn't know how or when I'd be able to properly use my newfound insights about giving, but I knew I wanted to. I returned home, and inspired by my new acquaintances and the suggestion of the KPI program, I set about writing my first book, *Doing IT For Money*. It took me 43 days from go to whoa to complete the manuscript.

The next four years were a blur as I began my own entrepreneurial journey, and I had the chance to meet and collaborate with many extraordinary people and businesses, culminating in an S&P/ASX 50 leadership role. If you'd told me in 2018 that I'd have written a bestselling book, joined the board of a small charity, lectured at Sydney University, spoken at the International Conference Centre in Sydney and Royal Melbourne Institute of Technology, and been a senior executive in industry, I wouldn't have believed you. And if you'd told me the world would all but shut up shop for eighteen months in the middle of all that as well because of a global pandemic, I'd have suggested medication might be a good idea.

Career 2.1

Yet here we are. I have done all of those things in what feels like no time, and I'm still only fifty-four. So what next for career two?

Well, I suppose it starts here, with this book. When I wrote *Doing IT*, as I refer to it, it was the book I could write at the time, a retrospective of my IT life to date. This book builds on that, incorporating the last four years and my newfound perspectives on giving and making an impact. *Doing IT* was a launchpad and helped me build a career talking about SaaS and software more widely. I'm optimistic this book will do the same, and I have grand ideas. You see, software does one thing that almost nothing else can: it binds us all together. It's the thread that connects our lives no matter where we are on this planet.

Billions of people are exposed to technology every day, whether at work, shopping, travelling, playing or whatever. And where others see scale, I see opportunity. A massive opportunity to unite humanity and leverage technology and our connection to make the world a better place.

It's a lofty ideal for sure, but if one is going to dream, one might as well dream big.

Still, there's a time and place to tell you about such things, and that means you'll have to wait until the end. By then you should have a far greater understanding of the world of software, and you'll be ready to merge the two. For now, however, it's time to get back to the core topic of SaaS and the roller-coaster that it is creating and owning software.

A STRUCTURED PERSPECTIVE

The many thousands of eager entrepreneurs starting new ventures will need to do more than simply follow a playbook if they wish to survive to maturity in what is likely to be a highly competitive market. What they need is perspective: a framework they can use to organise their thoughts and give them targets to aim at.

Mine is the 4Ps. Well, it was when I started writing this book, but it's now the 5Ps. As you're about to find out in the coming chapters, my world changed somewhat between the day I started writing and today and it's added an extra P. Still, I'll tell you all about that in due course.

For now, I'll stick to four.

Hopefully the idea that your software is only one part of the wider, more complex SaaS world is coming into focus, so you won't be surprised that the 4Ps only has one component directly related to it.

There are four pillars that support a successful SaaS business, and each one has three tenets:

- PEOPLE: Connect, customers and community
- PLATFORM: Solution, systems and strategy
- PROMOTION: Campaign, content and conversion
- PARTNERS: Flexibility, fluidity and focus

PEOPLE puts your prospects, customers, team and more front and centre, because human-centricity is key. It covers how you identify and connect with your target audience and how you ensure you find the best possible customers. And once you've got them, it encourages you to develop so much more than just some software, helping you create an ecosystem and community dedicated to delivering the best possible outcomes and service for your people.

PLATFORM refers to your core technology, the essence of your business, and it's based on your solution and development systems and strategy. It covers the needs of your software, from the early days of ideation and prototyping, through planning, development, minimal viable product, early adoption, release and finally ownership. It helps you understand the complexity and scale of the development lifecycle and it encourages you to focus on the needs of people at all times.

PROMOTE builds on your foundations, helping you develop a complete go-to-market strategy and sell your product. It looks at your campaigns and how you take your offering to market. It teaches you how to develop focused content that speaks directly to your target audience. Finally, it seals the deal, showing you how your complete offering will lead to the conversion of your prospects into happy and active members of your community.

PARTNERS are the final piece of the puzzle, offering your business flexibility, fluidity, and the chance to focus on what you do best. Rather than you doing everything, your partners allow you to scale almost on demand and they deliver financial stability through shared marketing and delivery costs. Lastly, they simplify your world, helping you market, sell and deliver your product, leaving you to concentrate on building a world-class platform.

WHAT'S NEXT

This structured approach is pertinent to all SaaS businesses large or small, and it will help you organise the many different topics you're about to read about. It's also a very valuable check and balance that you can use to make sure you've got your bases covered. But as this book is predominantly aimed at the up-and-coming SaaS entrepreneur, and some of you will still only be dreaming of your future, I'm going to start at the beginning and walk you through the SaaS world in a roughly chronological order, taking you from the moment of your first idea, through your preparation and getting ready to write some code, the building of your dream, going to market, and ownership of your up-and-coming software superstar.

And by the end you'll hopefully have learned that just like having a child, all that led to the moment of birth is nothing compared to the ongoing roller-coaster ride that is parenthood, whether it's your human or digital baby.

SUMMARY

By now, you should know that this is the right book for you and you're in the capable and expert hands of someone who's utterly passionate about all things software as a service and its world-changing potential.

So, if you'd like to share in my wealth of experience, find a few shortcuts, dodge a few of the slings and arrows of outrageous fortune, begin to unravel the massively complex world of software, and do it all in language that normal people have a decent chance of understanding, it's to time to get down to business.

Shall we?

Top SaaS tip: If you're looking at the technology, you're missing the point.

CHAPTER 2

BEFORE YOU START

Before you get on the roller-coaster.

Before you become emotionally attached to your idea and the potential it represents.

Before you give up a perfectly decent career and comfortable salary.

Before you refinance the house and gamble your nest egg.

Before you dig a huge financial hole.

Before you do something you and yours might regret.

Before you … [insert potentially life-changing moment here] …

… there are a few things you should probably know about the world I call my professional home.

While I absolutely love this place, and I'm deeply passionate about the technology industry and software in particular, this has been my comfortable place for a very long time. I love it to death, and I'd like you to too, but I'm not going to lie to you …

This is not a destination that suits everyone.

FAILURE IS DEFINITELY AN OPTION

The software world, like many others, is populated by successful people who'll tell you that had they known they were going to pay such a hefty price, they'd never have started. Similarly, we've all heard the world-famous rockstar telling of the teacher who said they'd never amount to anything. But, for everyone who made it big, there are many more whose successes in life have been far more modest.

So it is in the SaaS and software world.

Statistically speaking, roughly ten out of every eleven SaaS ventures are dead and buried within about three years. It's a chilling statistic, and one of my motivators for wearing my fingers to nubs writing this book. It's a number I'd very much like to change. It breaks my heart when I see good people with laudable ideals put their life savings – and even their homes – on the line for a shot at the title, only to lose everything.

I have stories aplenty, some of them truly tragic, and I'll share a few as we go. But for now, I'll just tell you that the software world is a wonderful place, but it can be utterly brutal and it's no place for naïve, unsuspecting tourists.

I'd like to say I don't want to turn you away from following your software dreams. I'd love nothing more than for you to make a great platform, change a few people's lives, have success and live happily ever after. And of course, there's some who will achieve that. But for some reading this, that's a very unlikely outcome. The stats are truly against you. For you, I want nothing more than to help you realise the end of the rainbow will always remain elusive. I want you to stay in the world you're in now. It might not be perfect. It might not fulfil your dreams. But it's safe, comfortable and – barring misfortune – it'll be really rather enjoyable.

Sorry to sound so negative, but I thought it best to get it out of the way early on. I'd much rather you put this book down now and said, 'You know, I think he's got a point', than spend eighteen months and a huge pile of money proving me right. Of course, if you are thinking of stopping reading now ... DON'T! You might just learn the one thing that makes the all-important difference.

Top SaaS tip: Only ever spend what you're prepared to lose – because there's a good chance you will.

COMMERCIAL-GRADE SOFTWARE DEVELOPMENT IS EXPENSIVE

I genuinely love the wide-eyed enthusiasm and optimism of SaaS founders. It is truly infectious. I'm fortunate that I speak with many around the world, and it's one of the highlights of my day-to-day existence.

I love their belief in their new, superlative 'mousetrap'. I love how they're going to sell it to the entire world, and how they'll help so many people. And I love their passion. It truly is a wonderful thing.

But there are a couple of things I don't like.

First is that so many simply don't understand how expensive the experience is going to be, and secondly, and perhaps more importantly, they don't understand why.

Making software is always more complicated and costly than we think. Even we hardened professionals get it wrong, and very wrong sometimes. When I was a developer, my rule of thumb was to work out how long I thought it would take, double it, and add a bit more for safety. And I still use that today when others give me their estimates.

It's far better in my experience to think something will take a year and have it delivered in half the time than to spend a very frustrating six months or so waiting, and paying, for a result. It can lead to lots of very poor behaviours, like cutting corners in the hope of accelerating the timeline.

That entrepreneurs often don't know why it's so expensive smacks of a failure to do proper research. And given that you're getting into a multi-million-dollar business, that could in certain lights be thought of as somewhat lax, to say the least.

Still, ignorance can be bliss. It's knowing that really hurts.

The harsh reality is that despite fifty years of mainstream programming, the industry is a little stuck in a rut. I'll delve a little deeper into tools in a while, but as we stand, development of commercial-grade software is largely a manual affair. This is not to say that there aren't options that make life a little easier for your team, but it's still a manual task. To use an old-fashioned word, it's a craft, so you need to think of your best developers as craftspeople.

Just as we would with someone like a carpenter or cabinetmaker, we hire such highly skilled individuals when we want a tailored solution; when we're striving for a high-quality finish; and when we want an outcome that's special or unique. We don't hire them to construct a flat pack from Ikea. Somebody from TaskRabbit can do that at a fraction of the cost.

Software development is expensive because commercial-grade comes at a premium, always takes longer than you think, and the bums on seats doing the toil are highly skilled people deserving of the dollars you put in their palms.

Well, most of them are. More on that later too.

What is 'commercial-grade' software?

My first programming job was creating reports for an insurance company. I wrote code to inspect the data stored in the corporate database and turn it into something understandable by humans. I also wrote simple tools to help people produce their own reports. Such things have a captive audience, and this gives developers a somewhat easier time. If something goes wrong, the IT department is only a phone call away. (This was so long ago we didn't have email.)

But the tools you use on your PC or Mac, like Windows or Microsoft Office, or the common SaaS platforms like Gmail, HubSpot and so on, have been created for an external audience. These platforms are generally far more complex and require a far greater level of rigour when it comes to development practices, the creation of help, training courses and more. Few commercial platforms are simple, and most are far more complex than people think. Browser-based applications are more complex still. They must work consistently in different browsers – such as Chrome or Firefox – which have subtly different requirements, and they must also work on different screen sizes, ranging from large monitors to tiny phones. That's something that might seem pretty straightforward if you're making a WordPress website, but when it's a real-world application there are far more problems to solve.

So 'commercial-grade' is a phrase I use to encompass all of the needs of a piece of software that's going out there to be used by the great unwashed, and as you might be beginning to suspect, complexity is hard to avoid.

> Top SaaS tip: If you're in the SaaS business, ignorance of the complications of software is no defence when there is a problem.

Seriously ... how expensive?

I hate to be evasive, but the answer is that I don't know, but you should assume it's going to be *a lot*, and that's with best practice, which certainly isn't common practice.

Trying to put a dollar amount on the creation of a platform is a difficult thing as there are so many variables, but by far your biggest expense will be your development team – these people can consume your dollars at an extraordinary rate. In Australia in 2022, if you were to simply employ a run-of-the-mill developer, you wouldn't get much change out of $120,000 per annum. And that's just an average developer, with limited if any real experience in application architecture, commercial design, project leadership and all the other good stuff you absolutely should invest in.

Hiring that developer as part of a team is okay. Hiring her on her own to do everything would be bad, and I mean really bad.

You might get lucky, but it's unlikely to end well.

If you outsource to a professional team, the same person will likely cost another 50% or so on top, but you'll be paying for the project as a whole, so you'll get more for your money. The question then is whether twelve worker-months is enough, and of course the more complex the problem to solve the longer it's going to take. You can safely assume at this point though that six months is an absolute minimum time to go from inception to commercial availability.

So, rounding up and adding on 20% because there are always variables, and then a little bit more for safety, and $150,000 per year seems like a reasonable, bare minimum starting point for a skilled developer. *One* skilled developer.

No more pay days

You must also factor in the cost of you not working at a regular day job. It's worthy of note that while you're busying yourself with the day-to-day activities of software creation, at least six months and probably a lot more are going to pass. That's six months of mortgage or rent payments, food, heating, keeping the car on the road and so on.

In short, you have to live.

Going into business for yourself is a big leap of faith. I know from experience. You leave a comfortable environment with regular money and a team around you, and march out into the light with little more than your wits and what you have in the bank. The trouble is, the latter of the two will start to dwindle rapidly, and that can quickly lead you to getting to the end of the former.

If your new career involves you selling your trade skills, you can start to earn a living very quickly. It might not be the kind of money you're used to or hope to earn, but it's something. If you open a shop, you get to spend a decent chunk up front on stock and fixtures and fittings, but you should at least have some customers as soon as you open and they'll start to provide an income.

When you're creating a SaaS platform, for a long time you get nada, zip, zilch, diddly-squat, bupkis, bugger-all and sweet Fanny Adams. In short, you get seven types of *nothing* until you've got a minimum viable product, and even then you still don't have any customers.

Some try to keep a job going and create their masterpiece as a side hustle, guaranteeing themselves exceptionally long days and plenty of stress. It also means they're spreading themselves thinly, making their work life far harder, personal life almost nonexistent, and not really focusing on the needs of the project.

It's not a path I'd choose, but each to their own.

Again, it's not that I want to dissuade you from having a go. I just want to make sure you know how deep the hole can be.

A CAUTIONARY TALE

To try to give you some perspective on how wrong this can go, I'll share a sadly true story with you of an entrepreneur I had some dealings with. I'll call him Alan.

Like many domain experts entering the SaaS world, Alan had recognised a problem, realised that his employer was spending millions of dollars to solve it, and thought he could build some software to address the issue.

Rather than telling his boss, in the best entrepreneurial tradition he kept this knowledge to himself, working on the basis that for $200,000 or so, he could get to market, save lots of businesses massive amounts of money and take a big slice of that for himself.

All good stuff so far.

Alan had some money in the bank he was prepared to take a flyer with, so he started down the path. He hired some developers and was quoted about $400,000 to build a minimum viable product. The trouble was though that while the software was relatively simple technically, the logic wasn't. It required a lot of complex maths and massive amounts of testing, and it soon became apparent that the initial estimate wasn't going to be enough.

Alan found some more money.

A few months later that was gone too, but significant advances had been made and the end point seemed attainable, so he begged, stole (not literally) and borrowed to raise more capital.

This time, progress was slower. The developers were struggling to resolve the issues, and as time went by, it became clearer and clearer they were out of their depth dealing with such specialised subject matter.

I met Alan when he'd spent nearly one million of his own dollars on a platform that at the time didn't work, and to all intents and purposes had absolutely no value whatsoever other than to him. He was going back to regular employment to earn some more money to continue chasing his dream.

THE MODERN GOLD RUSH

That's quite enough negativity for the moment, I think. It's time to move to the good stuff, with talk of making millions, buying helicopters and islands and so on.

And I've gotta say, if someone reads this and my advice helps them become super rich, I'll be happy as Larry, and he had a great deal to smile about. 'Larry' was Australian middleweight boxer Larry Foley, who in the 1890s won a grand prize of $150,000, which is equivalent to well over four million today. A New Zealand newspaper used the headline 'Happy as Larry', and the rest as they say is history.

Of course, many getting into SaaS today are jumping on the bandwagon. They're no different in many senses to the intrepid souls who chased their fortune in the many nineteenth-century gold rushes in the US, Australia, South Africa et al. Today, we're in the middle of the greatest technological advances in human history and we're only just beginning to scratch the surface. All you need is an idea of how you can help your fellow humans and some money to have a go, and you can make an internationally available software product and try to sell it to millions.

Becoming the next internet sensation is unlikely, but that doesn't mean you can't make a very comfortable living. The SaaS market is already huge, and it's growing, and growing, and is going to keep on growing for the foreseeable future. Cloud computing and the now all-but-ubiquitous internet have democratised technology, and with them has come a 'pile it high, sell it cheap' approach to software sales. Expensive tools that were once only available to big business are now standard fare for the millions of small businesses around the world. For example, small businesses can now use a file-sharing service such as Dropbox for a small monthly fee. Just a few years ago this functionality would have required a server costing hundreds of thousands of dollars, and regular IT support to run it.

HOW BIG IS THE MARKET?

According to some sources, expected revenues for 2023 could be as high as US$195 billion or so, and with a growth rate of 15% or more there's still plenty of meat left on the bone. This is underpinned by the adoption of SaaS platforms by, well, just about everyone. Consumers can't get enough, and while small businesses with fewer than fifty employees use about fifteen different products, the largest businesses have at least ten times that, and likely a lot more.

This has been exacerbated by the arrival of Covid-19 and the work-from-home phenomenon. This had such an impact on Australia that there was a shortage of hardware as businesses desperately tried to get their tech up to snuff. There was a shortage of desks and office chairs too, as everyone's spare room transformed overnight into their new office.

So $195 billion is a lot of money for sure. That's more than the gross domestic product generated by the forty-eight million people of Algeria in 2017. In fact, in just a few years from now, it's highly likely that only fifty countries worldwide will have a higher GDP than we're collectively spending on SaaS and cloud computing.

Now that's what I call a bandwagon!

I usually say that when you know there's a bandwagon, you're way too late. But this is one time when I might just reserve judgement for a while.

MOBILITY IS UBIQUITOUS

When my daughter was about eight, she asked how old I was when I got my first mobile phone. I told her I was twenty-eight. The look of confusion was so delightful, and I quickly explained to her that almost no one had their own phone before the mid-nineties.

What a long way we've come in just one human generation.

So pervasive are mobile devices today that even those in the poorest of nations have a decent chance of having access to one. In fact, in many places you're more likely to be connected to a mobile network than you are to what Western countries would regard as basic sanitation, primarily because mobile towers are far easier to construct than sewers, and they come with an almost immediate return on investment.

Ain't capitalism grand!

Over 60% of all people use the internet and over 90% of all internet traffic is through a mobile device. So, if you're selling a SaaS offering, you've got quite a few potential customers, and that's just the consumer market. There are millions of businesses around the world using the same tools too, and they've got far more money to spend.

COMPETITION IS FIERCE

Monstrously large as the market might be, the SaaS bandwagon bears a striking resemblance to a stereotypical train in India. Inside the first-class carriages, the seating is luxurious, the buffet car has excellent food, and the service is utterly delightful. But as we head towards the rear it gets fuller and the overcrowding begins. The seats are all taken; the floor is occupied; all alfresco options on the roof have been used, and everyone else is hanging on grimly to the side.

Yet the train keeps rolling on and more passengers seem to find their spot at every station.

In the SaaS world, competition for a place is just as fierce. Just a few years ago, there were few true SaaS platforms. Today there are many thousands, with more coming online almost daily. A quick search suggests there are thousands of marketing platforms, CRM (customer relationship management) tools and HR (human resources) products. And there are thousands of project management tools alone.

In fact, there seems to be a SaaS solution for just about everything – www.capterra.com lists hundreds of distinct categories. Not every one will be a pure SaaS product, but the majority will. Not that this should be a concern. Lots of competition is indicative of a healthy market and plenty of opportunity, so there's ample scope for some new players to stake their claim. And as I've already pointed out, and will likely repeat ad nauseam, if you're looking at the technology, you're missing the point.

WHAT SORT OF SAAS ARE YOU?

So, it's expensive, complicated, there's a cast of thousands out to get you, and it could all go terribly wrong, but I dare say you're still keen to have a go, so let's have a look at the different types of SaaS platforms.

Typically, SaaS is said to come in two types: horizontal and vertical. However, there is a third variety which is becoming more and more prevalent, especially in the business-to-business space, and I call these 'Service SaaS'. Each of the three demands its own perspective.

Horizontal

Horizontal offerings are the mass market, 'pile it high, sell it cheap' platforms that we're all familiar with like Gmail, Facebook, Calendly and so on. Here the product is very much the software itself, although that may not be how the business makes its money. Both Google and

Facebook make much of their revenue from paid advertising. And why not? They have an audience of billions worldwide.

Typically, these platforms are free and fairly simple to use, although there may be additional functionality available for a fee. LinkedIn is a good example. It's free for everyone, but there are paid options allowing you to search all of its 700+ million users and businesses, as well as providing other benefits.

In all these cases, it's the people themselves and the data they freely surrender that drives the revenue opportunities for the business. Whether you're targeting the mass market or not, that's a concept well worth tucking away in the back of your mind. It's going to play a big part in our technology future one way or another.

Vertical

Vertical or niche platforms usually solve a specific problem, like Atlassian's Jira which is used for issue tracking, or WiseTech's Cargowise, which optimises supply chains around the world. The software is still the product, and its sale and use is the primary source of revenue.

Typically, these products will be more complex, and can be far more expensive to buy. And by that, I mean that some of them are eye-wateringly and buttock-clenchingly pricey, and rightly so. They deliver massive value to a business, and if they're doing that, the vendor should be getting paid for it.

On top of that, and for the best outcomes, training will nearly always be required. While use of the software generates the lion's share of income, education and consultancy services provide additional lucrative activities.

Service SaaS

More and more businesses are creating platforms to help them deliver their service in a more efficient and effective manner. These often start as bespoke systems created for the business, but as the platform matures, an increasing number of self-service facilities are added until they get to a point where the customer can do much of, and maybe all, the work.

While this is in effect just a vertical niche product, the business is still primarily focused on delivering the service. A pure self-service option is just a cheap entry-level variant. As with vertical niche platforms, prices are usually comparatively high, and education is often a requirement.

I've worked with a number of vendors in this space in areas such as housing asset management, personal PR, debt recovery and more, and the complexity of the software is entirely dependent on the age of the platform and the specific industry.

WHAT SORT OF SAAS LEADER ARE YOU?

Speaking in broad terms, there are two types of people heading up SaaS businesses: technologists and domain experts.

Technologists

In short, people a bit like me. They probably come from an IT background and will be reasonably well versed in the goings on of the IT industry and all things computing. They may be experienced programmers, or will at least know something about writing code, and they'll feel very much at home tinkering with their PC or Mac when things don't quite go to plan.

However, the IT world is a big place and software design, and especially commercial application design, is a specialised role, and the skills that apply to one area don't necessarily translate to the software world.

I once worked with a former Microsoft engineer who had a PhD and patents to his name. He was a clever guy without a doubt, but when it came to the intricacies of the product we were working on, he was at a loss, and he struggled to translate his skills into something useful. Similarly, deposit me in the middle of a group of network engineers and I'd sink like a stone.

In my experience, technologists often struggle to keep out of the weeds, focusing on the technology and all the clever things they can do rather than on the problem at hand of building a commercial application. In the early days of a business, this is a valuable extra resource and can be extremely handy. But as time moves on, it can become increasingly necessary to rap them on the knuckles and tell them to mind their own business.

After all, why pay to have top talent make your product for you and then get in their way?

Domain experts

Like Alan in my earlier cautionary tale, most domain experts find themselves in the SaaS world because they recognised a problem in their industry or business and concluded that a software platform could help deliver a resolution.

Typically, they have little or no knowledge of computing beyond their day-to-day use of computers for their job. They may have some website design or programming skills, but they wouldn't consider themselves to be anything other than rank amateurs when it comes to technology.

While the technologists are getting lost in the technology, domain experts often get lost because of it. The moment they enter the software world, they find themselves surrounded by people speaking in tongues about subjects they have little to no experience of. It is in many senses a baptism of fire. Both groups are going to learn about commercialisation or internal selling in due course, but it's not an immediate requirement, so they get a run up to that.

The process of development starts in one form or another on day one.

The bad news for domain experts is that they need to start learning about it very quickly.

Top SaaS tip: Learn something new every day.

FAILING IS FUN

But only up to a point!

We learn early on in life that we can't win at everything, but most parents are kind enough to let us have an unearned victory or two. One of my few memories of my father, who died when I was ten, is of him letting me win at draughts, or checkers if you don't speak British

English. He had four kings and I had just one, but he very kindly lined them all up for me, and I jumped them all in one move. Of course, at such a tender age I had no idea of his generosity, and I joyfully ran off to tell mum that I'd just beaten him for the first time.

Just like my dad, the software world only affords us the occasional victory and learning to fail is something you'll need to get used to, and perhaps, dare I suggest, start learning to enjoy.

An early lesson

When I first started writing code professionally, I found that I was quite successful. I'd be given jobs and quite often I'd get to the end with few issues, and those were easily picked up in testing.

However, on one notable occasion, I was producing an extremely complex report that summarised insurance premiums by the risk type and another dimension that now escapes my memory.

The output was printed on continuous paper, the old-fashioned stuff with perforated holes down each side, and went on for many pages, perhaps fifty or so. As soon as it was done, I packed it off to the underwriting team, confident that I'd got it right. However, a couple of days later Bob came to see me and pointed to one figure in the middle of a page in the middle of the report and said there's no way that number's right.

In the midst of all the code I'd written was the simplest of mistakes. Just two simple lines of code in the wrong order. I hadn't reset a variable to zero, so it was carrying around an old value that was then adding into the total.

I fixed it and ran and printed the report again, and all was well.

At the time I just did what was necessary and moved on, but with the benefit of hindsight, I now realise that this was probably the first time my perfectionism really jumped out. I was genuinely pleased to have made something as perfect as I could.

The R&D way

In that environment, chasing perfection was relatively simple. But when I moved into commercial software, I was in for a rude awakening.

Simple it is not.

In fact, it's bloody complicated.

Reports are one thing, but applications with responsive user interfaces that work on different device sizes are in a different league. I failed every day, and multiple times. Rather than a simple green and black screen eighty characters wide and twenty-four deep, I was looking at 1024 pixels by 768. Today 1920 × 1080 is the norm and 4K and 8K screens are now available. And the applications do so much more.

In this world, you learn very quickly that failure is the normal state, and when you're inventing as you go, there is no 'right answer', just the one that's good enough for now. You may be working to a design brief, but these are only ever guidelines. In the software R&D space, you make something and then test it. Then you change a few things and try again … and again … and again … ad nauseam.

This is the R&D way and it's something you're going to need to come to terms with because user experience design is most definitely part artform. It's also one of the more time-consuming facets of software development. And there is a certain level of masochism involved with waking up every morning knowing that the fat bit of your day will be spent immersed in failure. Quite why I enjoyed it so much when it was my day to day, I don't know.

Good enough is good enough ... ?

Settling for less than perfection is a necessity. You must learn to be satisfied with something being 'good enough', and in the context of writing about failure I stand by this assertion.

You're going to suffer from a brief bout of cognitive dissonance later though, when I urge you to strive for quality in all you do and tell you that if you describe what you're looking at as 'good enough', it almost certainly isn't.

I know this from bitter experience.

I was asked by a development manager to review a new piece of functionality that Burt had put together – and he wasn't very good … at all. But being a polite young man and still relatively new to Australia, I was less than forthright.

I'm long past that now!

When pressed I said something like, 'Oh, it's good enough', which I thought came with some rather obvious implication and actually meant that he'd got the basics just about right, but the rest of it was a bag of crap.

Sadly, the nuance was lost, and the product was sent out.

It didn't go well!

This is of course British understatement of the highest calibre, and I was roundly lambasted for telling the boss that it was good enough when clearly it wasn't.

Top SaaS tip: Software R&D is the art of the compromise.

THE TOP NINE CONTRIBUTORS TO SAAS FAILURE

While the R&D process is most edifying and teaches us all a great deal about humility, it's probably worth me reminding you at this point that over 90% of new SaaS enterprises are dead in the water within three years or so.

Not surprisingly, there are many reasons why. Like aeroplane crashes, while it's the last mistake that ultimately causes the disaster, there are nearly always multiple contributory factors. As ever though, the stats are far from definitive, but they are suggestive of a pattern. So, the following are my top nine contributors to SaaS failure. Many of these will be covered in far greater detail later, so I'll shoot past at high speed and in no particular order for the moment.

Top SaaS tip: Implementation is everything.

Poor marketing

Rather than looking outwardly at the people and the problems it solves, marketing copy is often limited to the features of the product and what they do. If there's a malaise in the software industry, it's this.

Generally speaking, it's stuck in a rut that stretches back to the first internet bubble of the late 1990s.

It's an okay thing to do if you're the *only* platform in the space, but as there are likely hundreds just like yours, you won't be surprised to find that others do exactly the same as you. It's why car advertising doesn't talk about seatbelts, heaters and indicators. Everyone has them.

If you're looking at the technology … something, something …

Ignored customers

It's hard to understand why any software vendor would ignore their customers, but here we are. That said, there are many legitimate reasons as to why you shouldn't do everything the customer demands, but given that you're in the service industry, paying them scant regard is probably something to avoid.

Being outcompeted

As I've already mentioned, it's a competitive world. Some businesses will find they simply didn't do enough to distinguish themselves from their rivals, or get themselves in front of enough prospects, or run their sales well enough, or whatever.

There are winners and losers in every race.

Having a product but no business model

I see this one regularly, and it's a favourite failing of tech founders. They create a product because they think it is a promising idea, but they never really consider how they'll get it into the hands of the many customers they'll need to sustain themselves.

Happily, there's a whole chapter coming up about going to market. I'm sure this subject will be covered.

A user-unfriendly product

User experience, customer experience and human-centred design are hot topics at the moment, and rightly so. They are critical to success, although user experience is not as important as many people think. It turns out we humans are quite tolerant all in all, provided our efforts produce the results and value we want.

Pricing and cost issues

Many people think that SaaS is little more than software paid for via a subscription, and usually a fairly cheap one. But there's far more to it than that, and if there's a consistent issue I see, it's vendors setting their prices way too low.

It might be hard to believe right now, but there are at least twenty-five ways that good software adds value to a business, and probably a few more than that. Some might be hard to attach a dollar amount to, but they're still a way the customer can benefit.

Value is an interesting notion and deserving of greater investigation. I'll be sure to dig deeper later. (For those lacking in patience, it's in chapter six under the surprising heading of 'Value'.)

Having problems in the team

Friction between business founders is a problem at the best of times, and the SaaS world is no different. Throw in an extended time to get to market and massively increased costs in the early days, and it's no wonder so many run into problems.

Running out of cash

Part of my role when I work with SaaS businesses is to ensure they focus on the essentials rather than the superfluous. Every worker day of development in Australia is at least $500, so every worker month costs over $10,000, and it's easy to waste that and much more on work that can be done later.

No market need

This is the big one. Entrepreneurs are wasting literally hundreds of thousands of dollars on something that has no value (there it is again) to other people. And I'm not just talking about an isolated case. I come across such platforms with disturbing regularity, and the level of investment is just staggering.

Happily, there are lots of things you can do to make sure that the solution you're building isn't just some software looking for a problem to solve, so be sure to get out there and do some basic market validation.

SUCCESS IS DEFINITELY AN OPTION

I started the chapter by telling you that failure is most definitely an option, and it is.

But so is success.

So far, I've appraised you of the brutal nature of the SaaS world and the many, many ways it can all go terribly wrong, and I seem to have done a good job of that. But forewarned is forearmed, and I point these things out to raise awareness so that you can avoid the paths that aren't worth taking.

So, let's be a bit more positive now. If you understand the issues below it will go a long way towards making sure you survive your first five years, and beyond.

There are no silver bullets

And I should know. I've been making software for a long time now. If there's a dumb thing to do, I've probably done it. It seems like yesterday, but I made my first web application in the late 1990s. It was simplistic and utterly rubbish by modern standards of course, but the techniques and rationale behind its construction still hold true today.

They held true for years before it too.

This is an important thing for newly minted software entrepreneurs to understand because there's a stack of people just waiting for the opportunity to sell you something. Some will be other vendors hawking their products hoping to grab a slice of your pie, and others will be on your team telling you the latest and greatest something or other is the new must-have, perhaps in the hope that they'll get to add a new trendy offering to a resumé.

Whichever it might be, it's important to understand that the software industry advances incrementally just like any other. Software development hasn't really changed that much during my career. New tools have come and gone, and the browser and a slew of modern devices have presented us with new ways of delivering and consuming software, but at its core, software is still software, and it exists for one reason and one reason only.

It's a tool to help us solve a human problem.

This simple statement may come as a surprise, but it's true of all technology. Even the humble digging stick, one of man's earliest tools, was created for exactly this reason. We wanted to get to a root, so we created something that would help us. There's every chance we then turned it around and used it as a club to vanquish our enemies too, which is another common theme in our technological history.

So, software development today is just an improved version of all that's gone before, and today's generation of tools are only a small improvement on yesterday's.

Top SaaS tip: Beware the people who sell things for a living.

You must play the long game

Back in chapter one, I casually mentioned that success in SaaS comes when you play the long game, and this is one of the most important things I've written to date.

If you're thinking you might make a fast buck by knocking up a quick app, selling it to millions and then driving off into the sunset, it's highly likely you'll be disappointed and significantly poorer for the experience. For every Facebook or Angry Birds, there are countless others whose efforts never saw the light of day.

If you're in the software business today, you should be aiming to be in it ten years from now, and ideally, with many of the same customers. You might consider selling your burgeoning platform after a few years, but even then, you'll need to have built something serious. No sane investor will go near it if you haven't, and in the unlikely event that they do, they'll be offering a bargain price.

Focusing on the long game is essential for the simple reason that finding customers is not only hard, but also expensive. Depending on who you ask, it can be as much as twenty-five times more expensive to find a client than to keep one, so customer retention should be at the top of your list. And this is why I talk and write so much about service and the importance of 'the second S', as I call it.

If you want your customers to hang around, simply supplying decent software is only part of the solution. They're going to want a lot more than that to keep them satisfied. I'll write much more about that in the coming chapters, but I want you to understand early that the clever bit of your software, the bit where the magic happens, just ain't all that.

After all, you'll likely have at least ten, if not many more major competitors and you're all going to offer much the same functionality.

Don't forget the second S

No sooner have I mentioned it than here we are.

Let it never be said that I'm not a man of my word.

The service you wrap around the software is as important, if not more so, and getting it right will benefit you as well as the client, and of course, it starts long before they purchase anything. First impressions count, and even something as simple as adding a chatbot to your website can make a dramatic difference.

Remember, you're in competition with a raft of other vendors. Your prospects don't want you to be different. They want you to be better.

Okay, some don't, because they're cheapskates and will only ever buy based on price, but they're not the clients you're looking for. They can go about their business. Move along. (I like to throw in a Star Wars reference now and then. It reinforces the subtle nerd undertone I have going on.)

Service isn't about guaranteeing uptime and availability either, although they're considerations. Service is all about how you help, educate, support and so on. If you make the effort to look after your people at every turn, they'll forgive a surprising amount of your software sins. And that's a good thing, because one thing is for sure, you're going to have a whole heap of those in the early years.

I LEARNED THE HARD WAY

I'm sure there must be a pile of other stuff I should tell you before we get into the nitty gritty of creating, designing, building and selling software, but I'm excited to start writing about that, so I'm going to wrap up this chapter with a tale or two from the Marshall archives.

As I've already alluded to, you don't get to spend a career in R&D without stepping on a few landmines, and like any other expert in his or her field, there are many lessons to be learned along the way. Some are relatively small, like don't forward a customer email to a colleague with additional commentary that refers to the client as a 'pompous twat', and then realise you replied instead.

Oops!

Some are a little larger, and far more important, so here are my top three.

If you think it's going to be simple, think again

Software is like an iceberg. You only see a fraction of the whole. No matter how simple an idea might be, there are always thousands, or even millions, of moving parts that need to work together in perfect harmony.

I once, rather rashly, told my boss that a piece of work I was proposing would take two weeks or so. It seemed simple enough on the outside. But as ever, the devil was in the detail and in the end it took me twenty weeks.

Hey, at least I was half right. The first digit was on the money!

Mistakes are amplified at scale

This is one of the fundamental truths of software, and it applies equally to both how your application is coded and how it performs.

Quick and dirty fixes and poor bits of design may look innocuous at first, but the longer you own them and the more time and effort you spend working around them, the bigger the millstone you make for yourself.

Similarly, something that's almost perfect and running sweetly on your desk can look like the biggest pile of junk when it makes it into the real world. It's why testing with realistic and large amounts of data and concurrent users is so important.

I once made a screen that showed the results of a long-running process. To help the user, any errors that were produced were grouped together at the top. It worked very well for my few hundred. One of the testers tried many thousand and the whole application ground to a halt. It got stuck in a loop trying to update the screen, and while doing that further information was generated so it started trying to update the screen again.

If it's only in your head the project is dead

Unless you're going to do all the work yourself, you'll hire some software developers. This means you'll have to transfer every single ounce of knowledge, understanding, insight, dreams, desires and more from the well-formed interior of your mind to the as-yet unpopulated ones of the development team.

Writing it *all* down is the only option.

Unless you can articulate your vision in words and pictures they can understand, you're going to waste huge amounts of time, and given that even the allegedly cheap offshore variety of programmer most certainly isn't, every misunderstanding puts your project one step closer to disaster.

Sadly, I see this all the time, with young businesses forced to amend or even rewrite work they've only just completed because it just wasn't what the entrepreneur had in mind. I dealt with a shining example of this just a few weeks ago. When I asked about the specification used to guide the development process, I was told there wasn't one. They'd just let the developer make decisions as he'd gone along.

The results spoke for themselves, and very loudly.

Top SaaS tip: If you think it, INK IT!

SUMMARY

So here we are. The end of the beginning. I hope I've impressed upon you that this is no place for tourists and wantrepreneurs and that those who don't take this matter seriously are likely destined for a torrid time.

But for the brave, savvy, tenacious, committed, enthusiastic, entrepreneurial and prepared, the journey into the world of software can be a trip of a lifetime. You might set out to solve a problem, to earn a dollar and maybe even to strike it rich, and you may well get there, but it offers so much more than that.

The creation of software is the most human of endeavours, and once we stop looking at the technology and instead shift our attention to our people, their lives, and the value we can add for them and their people, we find that there is so much more to see than a few pixels on a screen.

And who knows, you might even transform some lives and make the world a better place.

You ready?

Top SaaS tip: Software is an exercise in empathy.

CHAPTER 3

PREPARATION, PREPARATION, PREPARATION

'There are no secrets to success. It is the result of preparation, hard work, and learning from failure.'

Colin Powell

As I've already discussed, regular failure is going to be something you'll come to accept – and perhaps even love in a strange kinda way – and I'm sure you're smart enough to learn from it. And hard work is something you're doubtless well used to, so there should be no problem there. So, if Colin is correct, all you need now is a little – or perhaps a lot – of preparation, and you'll be in the best position possible to take on the SaaS world.

You might also consider immersing yourself in research. Google, Bing and many other search engines will be more than happy to provide you with a list of thousands of articles, sources and opinions to read. I could recommend a few as I go, but I won't for the simple reason that I can't begin to choose, and most importantly the URLs change far too often. And when they do, people complain at me about the links being incorrect. So, I'll leave you to meander through a universe of content. If you stick to the mainstream, you won't go far wrong.

Right then, with that out of the way, here are the two most important things to get right.

WHAT'S THE PROBLEM AND WHOSE IS IT?

I think I've asked this question of just about every SaaS entrepreneur I've ever spoken with.

These are the two most important things for you to know because every facet of your business revolves around them. They should be the rationale behind the creation of your software platform and will guide your decisions from day one, and they will define the way you present your product to the market.

And if they're not, it's time to take a long hard look in the mirror.

In short, these are the two most important bits of information for you to know.

What's the problem?

It seems like the most obvious of questions, but many of the software owners I talk with find it hard to articulate the answer. Some have never even considered it. They just tell me what the platform does. That's a valuable piece of information of course, but it doesn't offer much by way of value.

Let's take the humble knife as an example. There are countless specialised versions the world over that have evolved to solve some specific problems. We have knives for surgery, butchery, cutting bread and so on. But if I hold up a scalpel, tell you it's very sharp and say it's used for cutting, you might try to use it to slice bread, and my guess is your morning toast might be a bit ragged.

Similarly, if I give a knife with a long, serrated blade to a surgeon and suggest he uses it on his next heart transplant patient, a funeral and lawsuit might not be too far away.

Knowing the problem gives you a far better chance of creating a tool that is specifically suited to the job at hand. It will help you focus your development efforts, target your resources and, perhaps best of all, those who have the problem will be far more likely to buy it. As you're in this to make a few dollars, that's something you should pay close attention to.

Whose is it?

Knowing the problem is part one, but problems aren't a *thing*. They have no physical form. They're an abstract construct, and they only manifest themselves when humans discover that something hasn't, doesn't or won't go quite as they desired or planned. They're very personal too. After all, one person's crisis can often be another's opportunity.

Your job then is to clearly identify who is suffering, and it's surprisingly easy to get that wrong. Consider the surgeon and his scalpel for a moment. If he were to use the bread knife, it would likely be detrimental to the health of the patient, but while ultimately the person under the knife has a rather bad day, she is not the one with the problem. The surgeon is. His problem is that he needs to make fine incisions to increase the likelihood of patient survival.

The same notions apply in the software world. The result of using a platform may be that a user has a far better experience, but the business delivering the service is the one with the problem to solve. It has customers who are unhappy and soon to be solving their own problems by receiving a better service elsewhere.

DEFINING YOUR NICHE

It's tempting at this stage to think in very broad terms about potential buyers, but I urge you to be extremely precise. If your platform will help small business owners, ask yourself which ones? There are over two million in Australia alone.

Do they all really have precisely the same problem?

I went through this process. While I can help SaaS vendors more broadly, I generally focus my efforts on domain experts coming into SaaS rather than technical founders, and vertical and service niche products rather than the mass-market solutions.

Knowing your niche allows you to articulate the problem more precisely and speak directly to those people affected by it. This will simplify your development greatly and sharpen your marketing and message when the time comes. Not only that, because you're targeting a certain group, you'll be able to charge more than you would for a generic offering.

To help you understand this, I'll recount the story used to educate me on the value of a niche.

Mark is a successful CEO and entrepreneur. One day he was doing some weight training at the gym when his bicep tendons detached. Unsurprisingly, he was keen to see a doctor, but he didn't want to see his GP. He wanted a specialist, a doctor who knew all about bicep tendons. Luckily, a leading consultant happened to be available, and Mark made a speedy recovery, far quicker than he would have had he used any old doctor.

And of course, the consultant, being someone with specialised and hyper-niche knowledge, charged like a wounded bull. He may not have had a hoard of patients, but those he had were very profitable.

So, as the old saying goes, the riches are in the niches.

I've just done a quick search on Google for 'tips for nailing your niche' and there are literally millions of results. I strongly suggest you take the time to understand your niche as early as possible. You may feel like you're limiting yourself, but what you're really doing is the reverse: you're beginning the process of winnowing out the chaff, and you can rest assured that there'll be plenty of that to get through.

Getting to the essence of your platform

So, knowing the *who* and *what* simplifies your world. It reduces confusion, saves on development and marketing costs and lets you charge more, and all of those are good for the bottom line. It improves customer satisfaction too. After all, you're making something just for them, and as you're playing the long game, that's got to be good.

What you need to understand now is what drives the purchaser.

There is an old sales story that says people don't buy drill bits, they buy the hole. That is to say that they are motivated to buy the drill bit because they really want the hole in the wall.

But is it that simple?

What are the holes for? A shelf?

If so, what's going to be put on it? Some family photos?

If so, who wants to put the pictures on display? A husband, wife, partner?

The drill bit gets bought in this case for something far more emotional than simply drilling a hole. This is a crucial thing to understand. Your target market is buying an outcome. They won't buy your software just because it's software. They'll buy it because it solves their problem, and in the process delivers something far more emotionally satisfying.

This is the essence of your platform. It's the core idea that you're taking to market. The more precisely you can articulate this notion today, the greater your chance of success tomorrow.

For example, I could tell you I help SaaS entrepreneurs create great software, and that's entirely true, albeit a little bland. I could zhoosh it up a little and say that I help SaaS entrepreneurs cut through the confusion, chaos and complication, so they can survive and thrive in the SaaS world.

If I'm trying to tug on a heart string and connect at an emotional level, what I say is that I help entrepreneurs create exceptional digital futures. And who wouldn't want one of those?

But I like to think big. And I mean really big. So today, I tell SaaS and business leaders that I help them create a global impact.

Now that's something to aspire to.

Top SaaS tip: The riches are in the niches.

FIRST STEPS

Understanding the problem you're solving and knowing who has it is a great start, but as I hope you know by now, you can't just knock up a bit of software and hope to get lucky. There's a lot of work to do to get a SaaS platform to market and it's my job to make sure you spend your resources in the best possible way, which is once and wisely. The good news here is that you don't need to spend any money just yet. Well, not the sort of money you're about to spend anyway.

Ignorance is no defence

In the coming months and years, you're going to spend lots of time talking with strange technologists who'll speak a different language about things you know next to nothing about. Such is the relationship between software writers and their paymasters. But let's think about that statement for minute.

I'm all for software developers improving their level of empathy. In my opinion, it's an area of the industry that can be massively improved. However, while we wait for Utopia to arrive we must deal with reality, and that means it's incumbent upon you to improve your knowledge and understanding of technology. This is not to say you should take a course in programming, although it may help, but more that you should ensure you're not one of those people who say they don't understand computers or how to use software.

As I've already said, SaaS is no place for tourists. Your opinion is going to be in high demand and the more you understand about the questions being asked of you and the contexts they apply to, the greater your chance of success. And as luck would have it, SaaS has made online learning a breeze. There is a profusion of short courses available today. I haven't taken any of them, so I can't recommend anything specifically, but Udemy has well over 2000 software-related beginner courses with many that can be completed in an afternoon and costing just a few dollars. And LinkedIn Learning is no slouch either.

Basically, you're spoilt for choice and have no excuse.

Sorry.

Write it down

I know it was only at the end of the previous chapter, a mere few pages ago, that I was suggesting you make the effort to write everything down, but I'm going to mention it again now in the hope of reinforcing the message.

The ideas you have are the most valuable commodity you own, but if you leave them locked away in your head, they're useless. At some point you're going to try to help a group of strangers understand everything you know, think, want, don't want, like, hate and so on.

Even better is if you can find something that looks like your vision. As ever, a picture paints a thousand words, so the more you can show them, the easier it will be.

It's a bit like a ...

I've been presented with many ideas. Some were well formed, cogent documents that clearly articulated the value, how the idea would work and how it would seamlessly fit in with and extend all that had gone before. Others were what we used to refer to as 'fag packet specs'.

'What's a fag packet spec?' I hear you cry.

Fag in this case is British slang for a cigarette. So a fag packet spec is usually a few often unintelligible scrawls on a small piece of paper, typically a cigarette packet, often written down while on a smoking break or Friday lunchtime in the pub, and usually with no discernible merit the following afternoon.

I received one a couple of years ago that contained a seven-page PowerPoint presentation of a few very poorly mocked up screens and a couple of short paragraphs about how it was going to revolutionise … something or other. The text included the statement, 'it's a bit like a checklist'. The sender was hoping I'd be able to turn their 'vision' into a technical specification, but with next to nothing to go on it was never going to be.

Such vagary does not serve anyone's purpose. If you're going to write it down, *write it down properly!* And I mean *everything!*

Twelve things to write down

EV-ER-Y-THING? Yes, *everything*.

Alright, *nearly* everything.

You don't need to drill down into explicit detail yet. There'll be plenty of opportunity for that later when constructing a spec, but if something has crossed your mind it's probably a pertinent idea, and especially if it relates to your domain knowledge.

Remember, the people who'll make your software will likely know nothing about your world. So, here's a dozen big ticket items you should start with:

- **The problem you're solving.** I know I'm being a bit repetitive, but here we are. It's important!
- **Whose problem it is.** This is important too.
- **The value it offers.** The more you know about your niche, the better you can understand the value. There are many ways to add value, so think in terms of money saved, issues avoided, opportunities created and so on.
- **Any specific functional requirements.** This is immensely helpful if you're a domain expert. You have to transfer your knowledge somehow.
- **What data will be stored.** Remember, you're the expert. Everyone else has no idea what you know or how you think.
- **How you envisage it working.** The more you can explain how it will work and deliver value, the easier it will be for others to help you.
- **How it integrates with other products.** Few platforms exist in isolation any more. How will yours connect to others, like accounting tools or CRM (customer relationship management) solutions?
- **A glossary of terms in plain English.** We IT people have our own vernacular, and so do you. Turn as much into plain English as you can.
- **Screenshots and links to competitor products in the same domain.** You'll have at least a 90% crossover with your competitors, so you might as well learn from the work they've already done.
- **Screenshots and links to products that work in a similar way.** There's absolutely nothing wrong with mimicking others.
- **Screenshots of sites with styling you like.** Understanding the aesthetic you're aiming for will help you visualise the final outcome.
- **Frequently asked questions.** If they're FAQs about your domain, they're going to come up again and again. Might as well write them down so that others can learn from you.

So, that's a dozen ideas, but the more you record the better off you'll be. This is really an exercise in starting to familiarise you with the intricacies of software development, and there are many. Happily, there's nothing here that requires anything more than a cursory understanding of software design, so you can start recording all of this long before you start working with a development team.

> **Top SaaS tip: Start with the assumption that the audience knows nothing.**

One hour, one week

All that preparation may sound like a lot of work, primarily because it is, but better your time now than a developer's later on. As the old wisdom tells us, prior preparation prevents poor performance, and there are few environments where that rings truer than software development. Anything you can do to pave the way for the professionals is time well spent and money saved, and as you get deeper into the project, where even a subtle change to the plan can result in many days and sometimes weeks of work, you'll truly appreciate the effort you put in up front.

My rule of thumb, and one of those oft-cited aphorisms, is that every hour spent planning and refining the details of the project will save one week of development time. The last thing you want is for your hard-earned budget to be spent on someone else's ignorance.

DREAMING OF THE BIG TIME

Doubtless while you're collecting and recording as much as you can, some of you will be fantasising about all the things you'll be able to buy and do once you become recognised in the market as a unicorn. These are the young businesses that the ever-opportunistic venture capitalists think will be worth a billion dollars.

Ahh … we can but dream.

Digital disruption

Still, opportunities abound in our modern world. We are in the midst of a technology revolution the likes of which we've never seen before, and there are many industries still waiting to be dragged, kicking and screaming, out of their historically analogue context. Those who commentate on such things tend to refer to this as 'digital disruption' or similar.

In reality though, digital disruption and its cousin digital transformation are little more than an extension of all that's been going on for the last fifty years or so, and precisely what I and many just like me have spent our careers doing. Whether that's something as simple as turning a previously printed report into an electronic facsimile or, at the other end of the scale, turning the taxi industry on its head as Uber has done, digital disruption and transformation are really just the application of modern technology to solve the problems of the day.

It may at times feel like revolution, but I can assure you the change has been entirely incremental and it's really just a rather rapid and exciting evolution.

Disruption essentials

This is an important idea for you as you start to flesh out your plans for world domination. The software you're building isn't going to change *everything*, just a few things, but if they're the right things the impact will be astonishing.

If you need an example of this, take some time out to read about Toyota's Kaizen approach, where continuous improvement means many tiny changes are implemented in their manufacturing process to ensure it's as efficient and productive as possible.

Of course, the challenge is to work out which areas to focus your effort on, and I think there are three guiding principles:

- **Be better.** 'Different isn't always better, but better is always different.' This is one of WiseTech Global CEO and billionaire software nerd Richard White's sayings.

  With the market as congested as it is, being different, having a unique selling point or offering an alternative simply isn't enough. What you offer has to be better, and that will likely take much more than just software, so don't waste your time on the superfluous. Find where you can deliver value.

There's that value thing again. It must be important.

- **Human-centricity.** Remember that it's not about the technology, but rather the outcome it produces, so focus on solving human problems.

  If the panic buying we saw repeatedly throughout Covid-19 has one lesson for us, it's that the interests of the individual are at the forefront of the buyer's mind. The greater good comes second and often by quite a distance.

  Your prospects will be asking themselves, 'What's in it for me?'

- **The 10%.** Delivering the 90% in your vertical is the minimum standard. It's your ticket to the dance.

  If you're to disrupt a market, the magic will be buried in the 10% that others are yet to tap into. And spoiler alert, it's not going to be one thing. It will likely be many.

Uber

To help you understand this, I'll use Uber as a perfect example of a service-based SaaS, one that leverages technology to deliver its service.

I had the pleasure of doing a couple of lectures at Sydney University, talking about all things innovation. One of the questions I posed at the end was, what was it that Uber did that made such a difference?

I wasn't the least bit surprised when the consensus answer was the app that we all install on our phones. After all, it's where the magic happens, right?

Actually, no. If we look beyond the glitzy exterior, it's really little more than a simple job allocator that replaces the surly dispatcher we used to speak to. Don't get me wrong – I like watching the car get closer on the map too, but after that, it really doesn't offer much beyond automated payments.

And it's this that gives us a clue.

Uber's secret ingredient is that it's made the experience for both the customer and the driver better.

The driver has customers who are no longer anonymous, which improves safety, and payment is guaranteed, rather than the previous risk of customers running away on arrival. Similarly, the customer has a driver who's no longer anonymous and journeys can be traced, both of which improve passenger safety and comfort. Add on the protected payments and the agreed price upfront and you have a far happier customer.

Both parties still get in a car and travel from A to B, but the process has been made simpler, safer and ultimately more enjoyable.

Stealth mode

Some of you will land upon genuinely brilliant and innovative ideas. However, few if any of them will be entirely unique, and most will be following in the footsteps of many that have gone before. While this might be construed as jumping on the bandwagon, it's worth noting that you can still make a very handsome living by taking a tiny slice out of a very big pie, especially if you can carve out a super-specialised niche and have your customers pay for the extra value you offer.

It's tempting then to keep your exploits a secret and hide away in the corner until the moment's right and you're ready to ambush your many competitors, but the more I see of this, the more I'm convinced it's predominantly a waste of time and energy.

I see this behaviour quite a lot. Entrepreneurs changing their LinkedIn profile to advertise that they're in stealth mode making something that's going to do something super-duper and change the lives of … whoever … yada yada. It's all very dramatic, clandestine and secretive, and all in all rather unnecessary.

This behaviour is driven by the fear that someone might run off with the idea, steal a march on them and corner the market, but this is an emotional response rather than a rational one.

The first issue here is that nearly all SaaS platforms will be joining an already crowded if not overflowing marketplace. And even if they are not, first-mover advantage isn't all it's cracked up to be, as I'll explain in a moment.

Secondly, commercial software as you're now doubtless aware is complicated, and if you're a domain expert digitising your expertise, it's going to be even more so. The chance of a competitor magically knocking something up almost overnight is slim, to say the least.

And thirdly, how many people can stop what they're doing and pivot to take on a new challenge they know next to nothing about that's going to cost a motza to implement?

So, hiding in the shadows is all rather paranoid really.

Of course, just because you're paranoid, it doesn't mean they're not out to get you – but seriously, enough with the cloak-and-dagger nonsense.

Incidentally, I'm of a similar opinion with regards to non-disclosure agreements. Clearly they have their place, and when there are squillions of dollars on the line they're likely a necessary evil, but the typical SaaS entrepreneur has minimal need of such complications.

First-mover ... advantage?

If you think you have something truly special, and you're breaking new ground and creating a new market, you could be the first to market.

Lucky you, right?

Maybe.

The trouble is, we've all been fed the line about first-mover advantage. This idea first appeared in a 1988 paper by David Montgomery from Stanford Business School, which he co-authored with Marvin Lieberman. In this they argued that being first to market was a good thing. Silicon Valley investors in the first internet bubble of the 1990s loved the idea and ran with it.

Many others are still running with it. I heard it trumpeted in a talk quite recently.

There's only one problem. This is a shining example of the idea that all that glitters isn't gold, and may actually be nothing more than the sparkly stuff that comes on Christmas decorations that you spend many frustrating weeks trying to rid yourself of once Twelfth Night has passed.

Subsequent research in 1993 by Peter Golder and Gerard Tellis suggested strongly that those who follow are more likely to survive, and in fact in 1998, Montgomery and Lieberman released another paper that walked back many of their original research claims.

Statistically speaking, of those first to market, nearly 50% will fail while over 90% of followers are likely to survive. Perhaps more importantly, those who come first typically end up with a smaller share of the market once the dust settles.

In the 1920s, Ford was churning out cars, enjoying 60% of the market while General Motors had just 6%. By the '30s the tables had turned. GM had over 30% and Ford only 28%.

And did you know that Google didn't invent Adwords? Two years before, the now long forgotten Goto.com was first in and best dressed. Don't feel too sorry for them though; they were bought out by Yahoo for US$1.6 billion, although that's notably a tiny fraction of Google's annual revenue.

There's a whole chapter coming up about going to market, but I wanted to make this point now.

Don't hide what you're doing. This is not to say that you should be advertising or shouting from the rooftops, but you can tell everyone about the essence of what you're doing and start to generate a little interest. Trust me on this one. You're going to need all the exposure you can get.

Top SaaS tip: There's nothing wrong with being a shameless self-promoter.

KEEPING YOUR CLIENTS ON SIDE

I'm sure by now you're full of ideas about how your software platform is going to solve the many problems of your many customers, and how you're all going to be the best of friends for many years to come. But to do this, you have to play the long game and find ways to keep your clients on side.

Broadly speaking, there are two ways you can achieve this.

Lock them in

This is a rather old-fashioned approach and one that's disappearing as technology becomes more democratised. It was a technique that vendors used way back when times were far less complicated and competitors far fewer.

There are two typical ploys.

The first is a long contract length. This means the buyer has to commit to the platform, making its purchase a far more strategic and therefore expensive decision and one that demands a far greater commitment in the early days. The idea that a prospect might like to try before buying wasn't really entertained.

The second was to make it difficult to move off the platform by making it hard to migrate data. Typically, this process would require many weeks of bespoke development to get it in the desired format, making it cost prohibitive.

I can't help but think that treating customers this way must generate a little ill will. It feels a bit like bullying to me.

Many large businesses still face these problems today, particularly when it comes to their core systems. It's why we hear stories of tens of millions being spent on a new solution. Some of it is licensing costs, but the lion's share goes on implementation and getting the business up to speed.

Set them free

Today, large corporate nightmare scenarios notwithstanding, the norm is to give clients as much latitude as possible. Rather than locking them in and holding their data to ransom, it's far easier for businesses to try before they buy, or to run pilot projects with no long-term commitments.

WiseTech Global, which is the de facto standard solution for supply chain optimisation and is used by 90% of the big players around the world, charges its customers on a usage basis. The more they use the platform, the more they pay, and vice versa. There are some long-term contracts, particularly for super-large customers, but many have just a short agreement to cover set up and getting up to speed.

Customers are then free to come and go as they please. They stay because the platform delivers value from the outset.

Top SaaS tip: If you love something, set it free.

THE SECOND S

Throughout this book, I'm going to bang on almost ad nauseam about the importance of the service you deliver, for the simple reason that it's the one thing you can use to really stand out.

Assuming a reasonably level playing field, most platforms will offer the same features. Just as most cars are just cars, so it is that most CRM (customer relationship management) platforms are, well, just CRMs. If you were to draw up a simple comparison list, you'd find that the features in one are the same as the features in the rest. There are of course a few differences, but by and large they're all much of a muchness.

Given this, how you treat and empower your customers becomes crucial to success. The more you can do for them the more they'll love you. The more you address their needs, the more value they'll get from the platform, the more they'll talk about it, the more likely they'll be to recommend it, the more they'll use it, the more … ah, you get the point.

Doing the MATHS

For me, there are five components to good service in the software world, and they're what I refer to as doing the MATHS. I'll write more about these later, but it's important that I raise these topics now because they're a fundamental part of your ecosystem and some of them need to be embedded within the software. Like any engineering, retrofitting is always far harder than building something in as you go.

MATHS in this case refers to maintenance, augmentation, training, help and support:

- **Maintenance.** You're going to have bugs, so fixing them will be part and parcel of your day-to-day existence.

- **Augmentation**. Software is never complete. It just gets bigger and better with age (just like the author!).

- **Training.** This is essential for all but the simplest of products, and will give your customers the best chance of early success. The more this can be aligned and integrated with the content of the platform the better.

- **Help.** High-quality documentation ensures your clients can find the answers to their problems without needing to wait for external assistance. As with training, the better this coordinates with the software, the better it is for all.

  Don't think of your documentation as something you write after the fact. It should be an integral part of the product.

- **Support.** When your customers need help, there should be a variety of options available, from community forums and email to phone support and more. For some, this will be the first port of call when they have a problem. For others, it will be the last.

Software *and* a service

The point I'm making here is that SaaS is really a bit of a misnomer. By calling it software *as* a service, the focus is on the technology, and as you now know this is somewhat missing the point.

In the highly interconnected and competitive global marketplace of today, selling access to some software merely gives you a ticket to the dance. You're just one of the crowd of potential suitors, and your many prospects are looking for so much more than just a nice smile.

If you want to be successful, how you treat them after you've taken their hand and led them to the dancefloor will be the deciding factor.

User vs customer experience

Thirty years ago, when I started my career, the ideas behind decent-quality graphical user interfaces were in their infancy, and there was minimal interest in the specifics of screen design. Sixteen-colour 'green and black' 24 × 80 devices were the mainstream, and such was the relative simplicity of the screen it was difficult to go wrong, though notably not impossible.

But in the 1990s Windows became the standard, and how best to organise the UI (user interface) became a hot issue. Microsoft even released a book on the subject called *The Windows Interface Guidelines*. While some of the specifics haven't aged well, most of the principles outlined still hold true.

Since then, the rise of the internet and the proliferation of devices has turned the user experience into an artform.

But while the user experience and UI design is important, and especially so for horizontal-niche, mass-market vendors, customer experience is where the rubber meets the road. Specialised platforms servicing tight vertical niches can get away with a lot when it comes to UI, and customers will give the vendor a fair amount of latitude, but treat them badly and they'll be gone.

And they won't be coming back ... ever.

Getting the customer experience right takes more than 'Doing the MATHS' though. These physical features are clearly necessary if you're to offer a complete environment but permeating them is something far less tangible. Quite what it is though is hard to define, and when I try to explain it, I always struggle.

Still, in for a penny and all that. So here goes.

It's the vibe

It's all about empathy.

If you'd told me ten years ago that I'd be talking about emotion in the context of software, I'd have suggested you give yourself a stern talking to. Today, I'll tell you that it's the secret ingredient. It's the magic something that will give you an edge.

What?

How does emotion fit into the brutally logical world of software?

Well, it's all to do with how you connect with your people. It's the language you use and how you communicate with clients within the product and outside, whether that's the text on the screen, training material, documentation, marketing copy or the scripts of your videos. It's the images you show and the colours you use.

It's the smiling, casually dressed professional woman in the twenty-five- to thirty-five-year age range on the Monday.com ad. She's their perfect customer avatar and it suggests strongly that Monday.com gets its people.

That's what I mean by empathy. When you understand your audience, what their problems are, what motivates them, what pleases them and how to communicate with them, you can mould your offering to their specific needs.

So, to paraphrase Dennis Denuto, 'In summing up … It's the vibe'.*

WHERE ARE YOU GETTING THE MONEY TO PAY FOR IT ALL?

So, you know the problem you're solving and whose it is, and you should have a reasonable idea of the primary value it will deliver for the customer. You have a sense of what it might look like, how it might work, the magnitude of the mountain you're about to climb, and you've got it all recorded ready to dump in front of one of those horribly expensive development partners I've been warning you about, unless of course you have the skills and time to do it all yourself.

Next question then.

Where are you getting the money to pay for it all?

Self-funding or bootstrapping

Whether you're a technically savvy SaaS leader who can do most of the planning and programming, or you're a domain expert reliant on a third party, you have a difficult choice to make. You can spend evenings, weekends and holidays hammering away feverishly at the keyboard while holding down a proper job that you care less and less about, or quit the comfortable nine to five and jump into the void headfirst and to hell with the consequences.

Either way, it comes at a price financially or emotionally, or maybe both, and it's a big commitment.

For many, the cash comes from savings or equity in a home. I've met a few entrepreneurs who've gone the whole nine yards and staked the family nest egg on their success, and I have to say, knowing all that I know about the SaaS world, it's not an option I'd choose. Others beg,

---

* Those not from Down Under should investigate this truly Antipodean cultural reference and watch *The Castle*. It's a magnificent piece of Australiana.

steal and borrow from family members and friends, often in exchange for equity in the business.

Grants

I can't talk with authority about other countries, but Australia has many government grants available, either at a federal or state level. This is not my area of expertise and the names and conditions of any specific initiative change regularly, so I'll avoid naming any.

As a general rule, getting in bed with government requires matched funding. If you want them to give you $100,000, you need to be able to demonstrate you have a similar amount available. Not only that, such money usually comes with a list of caveats, demands and other hoops to jump through, and you'll have the powers that be scrutinising your efforts, ensuring you toe the line.

Importantly, the grant money has been made available and it's highly likely that someone's going to benefit from it, so it might as well be you. I've also heard stories of grants that received no applications. So, why not apply? You've nothing to lose.

Investors

Then there's the venture capital community, and they differ from the government in one very big way: they're very much interested in a good result.

Renowned economist Milton Friedman describes the four ways of spending money. His fourth variant is 'other people's money on other people'. This is what governments do, and the result is they're far less interested in the outcomes. Provided the rules are being followed and they're being seen to be doing the right thing they're generally happy.

However, VCs are playing with their own money, or money entrusted to them by other wealthy and demanding parties. They don't give it out freely and they're very keen to see a return on their investment. A general rule of thumb here is that they're looking for a 1000% return, or ten times. Given the statistical likelihood of failure in the SaaS world, VCs are rather picky about the projects they get involved in, and not surprisingly, they'll drive a very hard bargain.

If you've ever watched *Dragon's Den* or *Shark Tank*, you'll know they're expecting some very well prepared and savvy entrepreneurs with well-defined business plans to pitch to them. One thing you can be sure of is the investors you're pitching to know you need the money far more than they need to be part of your business, and this puts them in a position of power and they know how to use it.

I won't use the rather crass description that a colleague of mine uses to describe the experience of getting into bed with such people, but bending over and lubricant are involved.

UNDERSTANDING AND ARTICULATING YOUR VALUE

Whoever you're approaching to help finance your adventure, being able to articulate your value is important, but it's an area that many entrepreneurs struggle with. I'll cover this in far greater detail when talking about going to market, but for now here are a couple of the big-ticket ideas that really show off the value of a solution.

Reduced running costs

For many businesses, lowering the wage bill and associated costs is seen as a panacea and is motivation enough to invest in technology. This is especially true in countries like Australia where wages are relatively high.

This is why warehouses use forklifts rather than peoplepower, a point I made in a lecture once, only for a young gentleman from India to point out that the same arguments don't necessarily apply in different locales. Apparently, his dad's business simply put a few guys on the truck and sent them along to do the hard work at the other end.

According to the Australian Bureau of Statistics, the average weekly salary in 2019 was about $1700. If we annualise that and add on the other costs like super contributions, the average annual cost of an employee exceeds $100,000. Still, I'm all for the simple life and nice round numbers, so let's call it $100,000 and move on.

If you can find a way to demonstrate that your platform could save a wage, that's a significant justification for using it. Of course, pointing out in a sales environment that a boss can make people redundant is a subject best avoided. It's probably a little better to point out they would have underutilised resources that could be spent on other profit-generating activities.

Reduced future costs

The flipside of the same argument is to demonstrate how much a business won't be spending in the future.

A system that costs one million dollars sounds like a lot. However, if that's over ten years, that's the same as employing just one person for the same amount of time and surely the software would do the work of far more people than that. It could be five, ten, twenty people, or perhaps even more.

If it's ten, that's a nine million dollar saving over ten years.

Better customer relations

Ever wondered why there are so many CRMs on the market?
There's a couple of reasons:

- The first is that it's not the most complex software, so it's a relatively easy market to get into.

- The second is that a well-used CRM delivers between $5 and $8 of value for every dollar invested by the user, because it improves the sales cycle and customer retention. This reduces marketing costs, improves customer lifetime value and so on, and anything that stops money going out the door is highly prized.

If your offering helps with any of those, its value can be huge.
Can you tell I hang out with sales teams from time to time?

DATA IS THE NEW GOLD

When I wrote my first book, *Doing IT for Money*, I wrote a section on the importance of data for businesses. It was the middle of 2018 and a staggering 58,000Gb of data was thought to be moving around the internet *every second*.

Here I am again a few years later, and that number has all but trebled. So, I'm going to repeat what I wrote then: 'Data is the new gold, and the more of it you have, the greater your level of opportunity.'

For most businesses, the data they collect is all about their business and their customers. This offers fantastic information about client behaviour, and if you have a sufficient quantity, modern data-mining techniques and artificial intelligence can offer extraordinary insights.

Even those with minimal data can gain valuable knowledge, and it can deliver excellent value. Something as simple as capturing the age range of your website visitors can change your perception of your target market and help you reduce your customer acquisition costs by letting you speak to a far smaller segment.

For most in the SaaS world though, there are twice as many opportunities, and massive potential, because not only do you have the data you're collecting about your clients, you may also have some of the data your clients are collecting too!

Platform data

When you think about the data you're going to collect, what do you think of?

The most obvious is the database that will store all the stuff necessary for your software. I'll use the CRM HubSpot as an example. HubSpot has a list of contacts, each with a name, phone number and so on, and you can also store company information. Being a CRM, it also records your activity, such as an email being sent or received, as well as the recipient opening and reading it. On top of that, it has a number of features to support marketing and sales automation, and each of those will need a place to store email templates, sales deals, tasks and much more. There are doubtless many more little sets of data that HubSpot records as it's going along.

These are the major data entities and their associated properties. Your development partner will help you through this stage when the time comes, but it's well worth you starting to get to grips with the requirements, especially if you're an expert in a domain that will be unfamiliar to most.

You'll be happy to know that there's minimal need for you to know anything about how or even where it's stored. Your development partners will sort that out for you too.

User and usage data

Then there's the user information used to sign in, account details, and a raft of metrics you can record to do with user behaviour. Which menu items are being clicked? What features of the product are being used? How long are they online? And so on.

Many modern applications ask if they can send anonymous user data to the vendor to help improve the product, and when you have thousands of users this is invaluable information. The more of it you can collect the better. Whether you have a use for it today is irrelevant. Record it anyway.

The Y2K (year two thousand) problems were caused when storage costs were astronomical, so they saved space by only storing the last two digits of a year. Today, data storage costs are negligible in the scheme of things.

Basically, there's no reason for you not to record every facet of your users' behaviour, and the more you know about that, the more equipped you are to help them solve their problems. Even if you can't see a use for it today, it may come in very handy many years from now.

> **Top SaaS tip: Record everything. You can always throw it away if you don't want it.**

CYBERSECURITY

Looking after your data is one of the most important aspects of SaaS ownership. This is not an optional extra and neither is doing the right thing by your customers.

If you'd like an object lesson in how to manage your ethical obligations badly, look no further than Facebook and Cambridge Analytica. Allowing a random third party to access millions of user profiles without their consent so that they can then on-sell the data to political parties is, well, let's just call it morally questionable.

When I think about it, it seems like it ought to have happened in the wild west days of the internet in the last millennium, but incredibly it was just a few short years ago. Happily, we have some new standards in place today and businesses the world over have obligations and legal frameworks to follow to ensure that user privacy is better managed.

The European Union has its General Data Protection Regulations (GDPR), which covers activity within the EU and the transfer of data outside of it, and at the time of writing around 75% of all nations have some kind of legislation or draft legislation designed to protect data, privacy and electronic information.

Those planning on collecting as much data as possible would be well advised to make sure their bases are covered and that their data is very well protected. The price for breaching these standards can be very hefty indeed. Equifax is perhaps the most notable example, with a fine of $575,000,000, and possibly even more, for its 2017 breach when the personal and financial data of 150,000,000 people was allowed out and about. Home Depot is still paying out for a breach that exposed fifty million credit card numbers and fifty-three million email addresses. The end total will likely exceed $200,000,000. Uber coughed up $160,000,000 when over fifty million user accounts were compromised. Apparently, Uber paid the bandits $100,000 to cover up the incident, but seemingly not well enough.

You may well be wondering how it is in these modern times that so much data is made available to so many by so few. Australia's Notifiable Data Breach stats have some valuable insights. It's only been going for a handful of years, but every quarter has remarkably similar stats. Around one-third can be directly attributed to human error, a handful to system errors, and the remaining almost two-thirds to something criminal or malicious.

That there are bad people out there looking to profit from your data isn't a surprise. The fact that good guys shoot themselves in the foot so often is. I'm sure there are lessons there to do with the importance of education, training, the development of processes and systems and so on, but this isn't really the time or place.

However, I strongly recommend that you take your cybersecurity responsibilities very seriously, and an annual review by a specialised provider is the minimum standard. Doubtless you'll have to spend a few grand for the service, but it's so much cheaper than the fines you'll face if you get caught out.

> **Top SaaS tip: Effective cybersecurity is a competitive advantage, not a cost.**

A cautionary tale

So, while I heartily endorse the collection of data, you should take note that despite it offering excellent value to your business, it also represents a massive risk, particularly if you're storing personal data.

In fact, while I was writing this book, Australia's second largest telco Optus reported that ten million customer records had been accessed illegally, including personal data such as passport numbers, driver's license data, health system data and more. Worse is that it appears to be a rather unsophisticated hack of data that should have been deleted long ago, and there are questions to be answered as to whether it should have been stored in the first place.

The incident is now being investigated by various government agencies, and Optus risks millions of dollars in fines. At two million dollars or so per contravention, the final bill could be monstrous.

But that's not the worst of it for them. The hacker posted the details of ten thousand customers on the internet and many nefarious groups have already started to use this for additional scams. Optus may well face a class action on top of whatever fines they receive when the dust finally settles.

To ice their particularly miserable cake, the CEO and perhaps some of the board may need to step down, and the cherry on the top will be the massive reputational damage. After all, who'd remain a customer after that, and who'd sign up for a new account?

I wonder how many rats are leaving what looks like a sinking ship too, guaranteeing a downturn in revenues?

PULLING THE TRIGGER

I'm a little amazed that I've filled two chapters with things for you to think about long before you do anything that's overly computer related, but that's how it should be. You might as well do as much as you can before you start haemorrhaging cash all over the place. Once you get on the roller-coaster, getting off isn't an option, and the SaaS world won't go easy on you just because you're the new kid.

A little prudence then will do you no harm at all.

So, I'll finish this chapter with my list of ten tips for SaaS startups. Some you'll recognise because I've already mentioned them, and others will become far more apparent in the coming pages.

Ten start-up tips

- **Know your what and who.** What problem are you solving and whose is it? Everything about your business will revolve around this simple premise.
- **If you think it, ink it.** The expensive people you're about to do business with need to know what you know, so write it all down.
- **Crystal clarity.** Have a clear picture of what you're making and the kind of value it will deliver.
- **Write it and do it once.** The more you plan, the more likely it is you'll only do anything once.
- **Know your data.** Capture it from the beginning because adding this in later is expensive.
- **Know your costs.** If you never get to market what you have is basically worthless, so be clear on your budget and what can you get for it.
- **Give users what they need.** Pare back your vision to the essentials. Bells and whistles can come when you can afford to waste money on them.
- **Stick to the plan.** It's why you made it. Any changes halfway through will hurt the budget.
- **You get what you pay for.** There are few if any shortcuts in the commercial software world, so do your homework and spend your resources once and wisely.

- **Make sure you've done the first nine tips.** If you have, and you're bored to tears with all the prep work and you just want to get on with actually making something, it's probably time to pull the trigger. But if you have any doubts … there's no rush. Another few weeks of crossing t's and dotting i's will do you no harm.

Top SaaS tip: Commercial software is the perfect environment for hastening slowly.

SUMMARY

Last chance to run away and live out a comfortable life.

No? Not for you?

Excellent!

By now, you should have done your homework. You should know what you're doing, where you're going and how you're going to pay for it. All that's left is the not insignificant task of turning all those brilliant ideas you have into commercial-grade software.

The best way I can describe how the next months and years of your life will feel is that it's a bit like becoming a parent for the first time. No matter how much preparation you do, no matter how many books you read or classes you go to, nothing quite prepares you for the reality of coming home with responsibility for a new life.

So, if you're ready to start making your new baby, and with strains of Marvin Gaye in the background, let's get it on.

Top SaaS tip: The more preparation you do, the luckier you'll be.

CHAPTER 4

READY, SET ...

Right then, it's time for some rubber to meet some road, and about the right time to start spending your hard-earned, begged, borrowed or hopefully not stolen cash.

But before you do, there's one more job. You have to find a development partner. And not that I want to put undue pressure on you, but this is your chance to completely fuck up your project before it's even off the ground.

Sorry to be so blunt, but there's a big pile of cash on the line and all programmers are not created equal, and neither are all software houses. There are some shockers out there, and horror stories abound. So, to get this chapter off to a nice cheery start, here's a cautionary tale.

ONE MORE CAUTIONARY TALE

Meet Julie. She's a lovely woman. Her name isn't real, but her story is.

Julie is a domain expert and some years ago she had an idea. And it was a good idea, one that would deliver exceptional value to her business customers by helping them improve their cashflow and cut down on debtors. She did her homework. She validated the market, picked a niche to aim at and so on. Julie did all the right things and her preparation prior to starting the build was admirable.

Then she picked the wrong development team. It wasn't her fault really. She thought she'd found the right people and that the school of hard knocks would teach her all she needed to know about the development process as she went along.

She was certainly right about that, but sadly, it was an expensive lesson.

What should have been a nine-month project and a minimum viable product for around $350,000 turned into 18 months and around $800,000.

It wasn't that the developers couldn't code, just that they'd never made anything so big. They simply lacked the experience and commercial rigour necessary, and the result was a poor design and a product that became impossible for them to maintain. In short, they were out of their depth, and with Julie being new to software, she had no way of knowing that the mess she saw was indicative of a far deeper problem.

So she stuck with them.

Reality started to hit home after six months or so when the list of bugs was getting bigger rather than smaller. Design problems plagued the user interface, caused by structural issues in the data model underpinning it, and attempts to fix one problem seemed to cause more than they resolved.

Eight months in and Julie and her development team parted ways. Hundreds of thousands spent on something with no value.

This tale does at least have a happy ending. Julie hired an expert to help her choose a second team, handing over all that had gone before. The new guys highlighted the issues they found. There were poor coding practices, almost no documentation, an obvious lack of teamwork and not a single test case had been written.

Julie and her new team have now built a useful product. She's gone to market and she's living her dream, but had she not had the finances to have a second shot, it would have all been for nought.

PICKING A DEVELOPMENT TEAM

Stories like Julie's are all too common, and few have the resources to come back from such a horrible beginning, so it's imperative that you invest time and effort when choosing a development partner. After all, you're about to get in bed with them for the foreseeable future, so finding a team that you're compatible with is essential.

If you think this sounds a little bit like a marriage, you're not far off.

Fifteen tips for picking a team

The problem with picking a development team is that it's hard enough even when you've been in the industry as long as I have. If you're new to it, it's just horrible. So, to help you along, here's my list of fifteen things you can do to help smooth the path. They're in no particular order, except for the first one.

I'm assuming you'll partner with a software house rather than employing a team directly, although you may well do that further down the line. Regardless, the rules apply equally to both scenarios.

- **Get expert help.** This is too big a decision and there's too much at stake for you to go it alone.
- **Use professionals.** Little nephew Jimmy may have shone like the sun when knocking up your WordPress website, but this is a different league.
- **Understand their core skillset.** Do they hand craft the code, use generators or high-speed tools, or something else? Whatever they create must be maintainable.
- **Get code samples.** At some point, you may want to hand over their work to a new team. Reviewing code samples will give you a sense of how well they structure their work. You may need to ask for help in this area.
- **Know how they run projects.** If they're any good, they'll be able to provide a detailed explanation of what they need to know and when.
- **Review project plans.** If they're any good, they'll show you previous plans and will be able to demonstrate how they walk the talk.
- **Review their portfolio.** There's little better than successful prior projects to inspire confidence. Take the time to look at other things they've built. Their output will speak volumes.

- **Find expertise in your space.** The more they know about what you do, the better it will be for all. It simplifies communications and minimises early design issues.

- **Fix the price.** You're paying for craftspeople to deliver value and it's going to come at a price. Hoping to get it on the cheap by paying for time might save you a few dollars, and it might not. And if it doesn't, every extra hour will feel like a dagger. Better then to know what you'll get and for how much, and have a few dollars left over to cover for the ironically predictable unexpected variables.

  In software development, surprises are rarely a good thing.

- **Determine how they communicate.** The best way to assess them is by being a pain in the rear. Call them, email, leave messages after hours and whatever else you can think to do. Find out how attentive they are and how well they explain themselves.

- **Obtain references.** Ask for some references and make sure you talk to them. Find out what was good and bad about dealing with them.

- **Understand how they work.** If you can, visit their office and find out how they work, how the team hangs together, how remote workers are enabled and so on. Software development is a team game and takes more than one person sitting in the corner.

- **Establish their depth.** How big is their team? What happens if your project lead takes a job elsewhere or gets sick? You're paying for an outcome, and they'll need to be able to fill the gap quickly.

- **Establish plain English communication.** Developers quite rightly have a reputation for speaking in gobbledegook. It is, in my experience, one of the biggest issues the industry faces. If they can't speak to you in non-technical language about your problem, it's probably time to try the next team.

- **Press pause.** The wrong decision will end your dream all too quickly, so if you have any doubts, press the pause button. Your idea will wait for a few months while you find the right team.

Top SaaS tip: The first answer isn't necessarily the right
answer.

Once you have your team, they'll be able to guide you through the
emotional turmoil that is software creation, and their expertise will
likely guide your choice of techniques and tools. You may never need
to know anything about this, but just in case, here's a quick overview of
the choices available to you.

CHOOSING THE RIGHT TOOLS

There are literally hundreds of tools your development team can use
to solve your problem, and there are shiny new distractions hitting
the market with alarming regularity. Some will become popular, and
others may simply wither and die on the vine.

The problem is that the long-term success of a tool isn't guaranteed.
Even major vendors like Microsoft have created products that looked
the part but never really gained traction. In 2007, Microsoft Silverlight
was released. It promised a great deal for browser applications, but
never quite made the grade and it was officially dead by the end of 2021.

Your team will have favourites, and that can sometimes spill over
into zealot-like religious belief of software superiority, but provided
they're using mainstream offerings of the day, you'll probably be in as
good a position as it's possible to be.

Development tools fall roughly into three different camps.

3GLs (third-generation languages)

These are the mainstream development tools you'll hear about, like
C# (C Sharp), HTML, JavaScript and Python. They're accompanied by
a slew of supporting products and libraries and prebuilt solutions to
common problems that help simplify the development process. These
addons tend to have the most volatile lifespans.

3GLs provide developers with the greatest flexibility because
they're intended to be used for a wide variety of solutions, and as a

result require the most effort to get the job done. As they're the mainstream, they're incredibly popular and finding people who know them is comparatively simple.

The downside with using such tools is they require the most effort and it will take longer to achieve the desired outcome, although this is improving every year.

Low code

Over the years, a variety of 4GLs (fourth-generation languages) have been developed. I spent much of my career helping to create one called LANSA. These were once referred to as CASE tools (computer-aided software engineering) and today are often referred to as low-code tools.

The idea behind low-code is simple. Much of what's done is repetitive, so it must be possible to simplify these actions and create building blocks and automated tools to do the work. Rather than trying to solve all possible development issues, they tend to focus on more common activities, like building business systems. This simplifies the development process and shortens the time to market.

The downside is these are far less popular and finding resources can be a problem. However, such tools are on the rise at the time of writing and they may offer a suitable solution for you. Because they automate many time-consuming activities and minimise the number of errors during programming, development times can be significantly reduced, saving you a big pile of cash.

OutSystems is another of the market leaders in this space and well worth investigation.

No code

The idea of the average person on the street developing software is a panacea that refuses to go away, and today there are many tools that require no specific programming knowledge. These offer great value for those with a limited budget who want to have a crack at building something.

However, all that glitters ain't gold, and as with any generic tool what you generally get is a generic outcome. This may cover 80% or 90% of what you need to create, but the remaining 10% is likely to hurt.

Compromise will of course be the key here, but it may also be that you need to engage in low-level development to deal with the remainder.

How much control you have over the application created for you will depend entirely on the tool. You should also bear in mind that you should be playing the long game, so future development requirements must be taken into consideration.

As I write, Bubble is one of the better no-code platforms.

Configurable websites

WordPress, on which over 40% of all websites are built, offers all manner of extensions for all manner of requirements. If your idea is very much like someone else's – for example, yet another dating app – there's a fair to middling chance that another wannabe SaaS vendor has already decided there's a dollar or two to be made by making a generic version and selling that to people just like you.

There are also a massive number of prebuilt configurable solutions where you simply add your own branding, text and images, and then link it to your own domain name and hey presto, you're up and running for a few hundred dollars.

Of course, reality is as ever that you get what you pay for. This may be enough to make a start, but it's likely not a long-term solution for serious SaaS players.

Another cautionary tale

Paul was the CTO (Chief Technology Officer) for a relatively new SaaS start-up. They were going well all in all, collecting customers, increasing revenues and generally doing all the things one would expect of a start-up heading in the right direction.

There was, however, one tiny little fly in the ointment.

They'd built their platform using a generic low-code tool. This had performed well in the early stages, but as the application grew in complexity and some of the screens became increasingly functional, they began to notice performance issues. What started out as sub-second response times soon became three or four seconds. Then six, eight, and by the time we spoke it was as long as twelve seconds before the screen would update.

Such response times are wholly unacceptable for most users and they risked losing some of their major accounts.

Paul had complained to the vendor of the tool but to little avail, and they had reached the point where they were seriously considering a complete and very expensive and resource-hungry rewrite using industry-standard tools so that they had complete control in the future.

As Paul said to me at the time, 'It's not end of the world, but I think I can see it from here.'

*

How do you pick?

Whether native tools, low code or no code is right for you will depend on budget, skills availability and the nature of the application. As a rule of thumb, using industry-standard 3GL tools is the right answer. This will give you complete control over everything you do, and you're likely going to need that as you scale and grow the business.

However, if one plans to be a world swimming champion it's important not drown at the start of your career. Coding at a lower level consumes more resources. More time, more money, more patience. You will need to determine whether you have enough of each to be able to get to market.

I strongly recommend you gain some objective help on this one. Your future survival may well depend on the decision you make.

Top SaaS tip: Pick the team then the tool.

THE PROBLEM WITH PROGRAMMING

Maurice Wilkes, an early computing pioneer and the inventor of microprogramming, once said, 'As soon as we started programming, we found out to our surprise that it wasn't as easy to get programs right as we had thought.'

Hmm … no shit!

That was true in the 1950s and it's still true today. Despite 70 years of progress, the trials and tribulations of software creators remain much as they have always been. Low-code tools may have solved some of the problems, but the sheer complexity of large systems means that many programmers are simply not equipped to deal with them. They may be able to read the code but understanding what it means is beyond them until someone familiar with it gives them some context. And even then, it can take a while for the many pennies to collectively drop.

Make the system big enough and it can take many months for new team members to get up to speed.

As your platform evolves over the coming years, you'll run into the same issues.

Isn't it just logic?

Yes, it is. It's just a series of instructions, except that there can be literally millions of them, and the context that they apply to is all important.

Firstly, there's data. Anyone who's ever used a spreadsheet in anger will understand the challenges of dealing with two or more sets of related information. Now scale that to a commercial system where there may be hundreds of tables, with many dependent on others, and each with many columns. It can get very messy very quickly, which is why database design skills are so important.

Then there are the rules that govern what data is permissible. This must be implemented rigorously, and simply defining them in the first place demands specialist knowledge of the subject matter.

Lastly, well for this simple overview, there's the user interface. Today, that must be aesthetically pleasing, work effectively on multiple screen sizes, handle touch and pointer control, follow all the rules of the data, and so on.

It's a team game

With so many tools, databases, domain knowledge requirements, many other specialist skills that I won't even begin to mention, and an almost infinite variety of user interface demands, it's highly unlikely you'll find one person who can solve your problem for you.

Realistically, it takes a team, and this is why I recommend that rather than trying to hire a group of individuals, you instead seek out a development partner. They should have a wide variety of skills, and even if they don't have something you need, they'll have a network of supporting players who'll be able to jump in.

Sadly, I've seen more than enough projects derailed by internal development issues to know that outsourcing in the early days is most likely to produce the right results. More often than not, it's a two-person team with a domain expert and a developer. It all seems easy enough in the first few weeks, but the magnitude of the job can easily overwhelm a single person. Rapid progress in the first few months slows to a snail's pace as the devil in the detail becomes apparent.

And once the pace drops, picking it back up is awfully hard.

WRITING A SPECIFICATION

Remember all that stuff I urged you to write down? All those wishes and dreams?

It's about to come in handy.

You and your new best friends in the development shop are about to turn it into a functional specification. The good news for you is that they'll do the majority of the legwork here. After all, they are the experts. Your job is to make sure what they come up with fits in with what you envisaged, and most of all, to ensure everything you want is included, and what you don't isn't.

Whatever ends up in the spec is what you're going to get for your money. If what's in there is wrong, it's on you. If what's in there is right and they make it wrong, it's on them. So it's in your collective best interests to ensure there's no ambiguity in the language you both use. Perfection as ever is hard to achieve, so to help smooth the path, I strongly recommend the creation of a glossary of terms. This is particularly valuable when dealing with niche domain knowledge because it's unlikely that the developers will understand the language you use, just as you might not understand them.

You also have the not so simple task of ensuring your own data integrity. Defining functional requirements and coming up with an appealing aesthetic, while far from straightforward, isn't overly tricky. Making sure that the rules for your data and business are followed is.

Broadly speaking, a spec has three parts that describe the data, the functionality and the user experience, or what we used to refer to as the look and feel.

The data

If you've done your preparation well, you should have a good grasp of the kind of data you want to collect, and if you've been super diligent, you'll have a very detailed understanding of it. If you haven't, the dev team will help you through the process, but it's a good idea to be as ready as possible.

Accuracy at this point is critical. This is foundational stuff, so anything wrong here will affect all that follows, and as the person helping you write the spec is unlikely to write the code, it's best that you both pay close attention to the problem at hand and ensure you're on the same page.

To help you understand the process a little, here's a relatively simple example of how the details can drive complexity, even in what appears to a very simple scenario.

Entities and elements

Suppose you want to store something we're all familiar with, like contact information. You might perhaps take a moment here to look at the Contact app on your phone so you can see what I'm on about.

In its simplest form, we might have a Name, Address, Phone Number and Email. So, that's one entity, Contact, and four elements, or attributes – the specific little bits of data we store about something.

However, Name is typically split into FirstName and Surname or FamilyName, and Address will likely have a StreetNumber, StreetName, Suburb, Town, State, Country and Postcode.

That's now one entity and eleven elements and nothing overly troublesome.

Now let's think about phone numbers. Many people have a mobile number, home, work mobile and more. In fact, the Apple Contacts app lists ten distinct types. So, each phone number needs two attributes to describe it: the number itself and the type of number. If we're to try to store that in a spreadsheet, we'd have 10 columns, one for each type of phone number, most of which would be blank for any given entry. This is an inefficient way to store the data, and becomes increasingly so every time we come up with a new type of phone number because we need to add another column.

The solution is to create a second entity which I'll inventively call PhoneNumber. A PhoneNumber has two elements, Type and Number. Instead of a Contact having a PhoneNumber element, it will now be called PhoneNumbers, because it represents one or more, and it will hold multiple child instances of a PhoneNumber.

The same problem applies to email addresses too, or a physical home and delivery address.

If this is all getting way too deep in the weeds, that's okay. No one, and least of all me, expects you to become an expert overnight. For simplicity, you can write down Phone Numbers as an element and your dev partner will sort out the details for you.

My aim here, as is the case with much of what I'm writing, is to give you an insight into the sorts of things that go on and to help you understand why seemingly simple changes can lead to significant repercussions, and as you can see, data structures become very complex, very quickly.

By the time we get to enterprise platforms, databases regularly have over one thousand tables to store data. And I haven't even told you about the good stuff, like third and fourth normal form and managing descriptions in multiple languages.

Happily, you can probably remain blissfully ignorant about those, for now.

Data integrity

For the uninitiated, data storage models are enough to make your head spin, and you'd be forgiven for doing your best owl impression or going the full Linda Blair in *The Exorcist*. Sorry to say, but the next stage of defining all the rules of behaviour will do little to calm your nerves.

To continue with the Contact example, we might want to make sure a name is recorded, but which one? Well, practicality must come in to play here. In a perfect world we'd want both, but if we mandate entry of the Surname, the user will have to put something in, whether they know it or not, and FirstName is no different. So, the rule seems to be that either FirstName or Surname must have a value for the data to be valid.

Or does it?

There might be a legitimate scenario where both being blank is acceptable. For example, we might want to create a contact because we have an email address and a phone number, but we don't yet know whose they are. Situations like this are fairly common and largely a pragmatic response to the needs of the user.

Determining what's allowable is all part and parcel of designing the application, and you'll find as you go through the development process that a few of the hard and fast rules you think make complete sense are instead rather annoying when trying to use the tools you've created.

Managing the multiple email addresses is even more interesting. Firstly, there's the Type of Email – Home, Work and so on. If we hard code the Type in the program code, we're setting ourselves up for a maintenance problem. Every time we create a new allowable Type or change its name – for example, from Work to Business – we have to find all the places where email Type is used and change it.

Best practice in cases such as this is to store a list of the allowable values and refer to that whenever there's a need, the idea being that it only exists in one place, so there's only one thing to change when the time comes.

Then there's the email address itself. How do we ensure that it's valid? The first problem is we need to ensure it follows the syntax rules for an email address. As humans, we generally know what one looks like. It has a first bit, then an @, then a domain; for example, sample@somewhere.com.au

However, that's only scratching the surface. If you'd really like to kill a few brain cells, search for email validation rules on Google and then follow the link to the Wikipedia page. I can tell you from personal experience, it's enough to make a grown man angry … very angry. Somewhere, in the darker recesses of the internet, there are threads dedicated to slanging matches about this stuff.

And even if the value adheres to the syntactic requirements for an email address, how do we know the email address exists and isn't just a typo: smaple@somewhere.com.au rather than sample@somewhere.com.au?

Happily, many others, including your dev team, have asked these questions before and the internet is awash with examples of how to manage such scenarios.

As you're beginning to see, there are hundreds of tiny decisions to make as you trundle through the design phase, and the more you can get right now, the simpler life will be later. Once you start writing code, changes to the data structure become increasingly troublesome, so it's better to talk through any concerns you have sooner rather than later.

Top SaaS tip: An hour of planning saves a week of work.

Designing a database is far from simple, and if you find this section a little hard to get to grips with, you're in good company. When I first started out, it was gibberish to me too. My point here isn't to teach you the finer points of application data design, but rather to highlight some of the issues you're going to run in to as you try to piece together the rules and regulations for your platform.

The functionality

Once you know the data that's in play, working out the functionality is a little easier. The simplest way to look at it is to think in terms of the actions your users will perform. Entities and elements use nouns to describe them, so actions, rather unsurprisingly, use verbs.

Continuing with the contact example, the application needs to be able to Create, Update and Delete a Contact. That looks like it covers all the bases, but computer people also talk about Reading data, which is to say that it's displayed on the screen without the ability to make a change, so there's a fourth variant.

This basic set of actions comprises what we loosely refer to as a CRUD (create, read, update, delete), and most business applications look pretty much like this once you get down to bare bones.

But of course, life is rarely if ever that simple, and software certainly isn't. If we want to help our users a bit more, we provide options to Send the contact details to someone else or Call the contact using the number entered, Email them, or perhaps Show a map of their address, and more. These all seem easy enough, and it's probably not too hard to imagine a screen showing the details of a Contact with some icons or a menu at the top with an appropriate set of options.

However, this is a simplistic example. Each action is discrete and merely starts an unrelated process. In reality, many of the actions attached to an entity change its state and perform far more complicated bits of processing.

Complex processes

To help explain this, I'll use another familiar concept, the online shopping cart, as an example. When using a site like Amazon, we can click on a product to see its details, and should we want something, we click Buy and the item is added to our cart. When we've finished, we choose to Checkout our goods and then we fill in delivery information, provide payment details and complete the transaction.

Somewhere in that process, our cart turns into an order that's transferred to a warehouse ready for fulfillment, money is charged using the appropriate payment gateway, the cart is emptied ready for the next time, data will be added to the accounting systems, various usage metrics will be recorded, and the list goes on. These complex processes need to be defined and then refined. To do this, you need to understand the business model, the data you're using and how it's affected by each action.

Delete doesn't always mean delete

A good example of this is the idea of deleting something. Pencils have erasers so that when we make a mistake, we can rub it out. Similarly, in the Word document I'm editing right now, my ham-fisted typing is easily and regularly corrected by use of backspace, delete or undo.

I use these a lot, and more so when people are watching. Marshall's law of keyboard skills states that one's ability to type is inversely proportional to the number of eyes watching.

In both prior cases the deletion is permanent, undo notwithstanding.

However, when we delete something in a complex application, in many cases we don't actually delete a database record. Instead, we simply add an element to indicate whether we consider it active, deleted, pending or whatever other states we can determine. We do this because there are many tables in a typical application database and some will contain additional data relating to the stuff we're trying to delete, and historical information is always handy so we keep it around.

For example, we might have an HR (human resources) application. If we really delete an employee when they leave, what do we do with all the ageing payroll records related to them? We would likely want to keep them (and may even be legally required to), but if we delete the main employee record, we have no way of knowing which employee the payroll data relates to.

Whether you can really delete something or not will depend entirely on the context and your particular needs and wants.

The right to be forgotten

One of the issues with saving just about everything for just about forever is, well, precisely that: it's forever. But not everyone wants their stuff to hang around like a bad smell, particularly if what's been saved is traumatic, embarrassing, or of potential interest to various government departments and best kept quiet.

To ensure a reasonably level playing field, there are now statutes in place that defend individual freedoms, such as the GDPR (the General Data Protection Regulations) in Europe. But that's just the EU – there are many different ordinances around the world.

But even someone's desire to disappear isn't necessarily enough to make us actually delete the data. Instead, we might anonymise it, replacing a name with something generic like 'Deleted Customer 123456'.

The user experience (UX)

When it comes to designing aesthetically appealing websites and the like, yours truly is far too close to being completely out of his depth for comfort. In the modern world, such things generally require professionals with artistic flair, graphic design skills, and highfalutin titles like User Experience Designer.

And that just isn't me. I'm somewhat lacking in such skills, although I'm well versed in the principles.

However, application user experience isn't just about sparkly graphics and picking an appropriate colour palette. In fact, beyond coming up with a basic design and setting a few ground rules, there's no need to do too much work in this area in the early stages. Modern development techniques should allow for a lot of this to be changed afterwards with minimal impact.

In its simplest form, you can think of this a bit like using styles in Word. Blocks of text are flagged as using a particular style – such as Heading 1 – and once the document is completed, you can change the definition of the style and all the places where it's used will magically update. You may need to tinker here or there if font sizes change but changing colours, bold, underline and so on is simple.

Sadly, there's a great deal more to it, but we need to start somewhere.

Whether we call it human-centred design, human-centricity, empathy or whatever, putting people in the middle and building your platform around their foibles is very much in vogue. It's also a highly subjective area. The good news is that people with far more talent and experience in this space have done this to death and I strongly recommend a little external research. And as ever, Google is there to deliver many more millions of blogs and sites where the illuminati are plying their trade.

However, for completeness, I'll include a little bit here, just to give you a taster.

In its simplest form, user experience comprises two things:

- the appearance of your platform
- its usability.

Keeping up appearances ... or not

In the good old days (oh, how I miss them), when IBM was still the dominant player, we had the CUA (common user access) guidelines and getting the appearance right was simple enough. There were only 16 colours for a start. I'm sure they were far more complex than this, but basically they said make sure everything lines up properly and use consistent function keys everywhere. F3 was Exit, F12 was Cancel, F21 (Shift + F9) put the screen in to edit mode, and so on.

F5 was typically used for Refresh as well, and that's still the same function key used in modern browsers to cause a web page to reload.

Who said my old skills are useless?

Today, having a strong aesthetic is important, and particularly so if you're in a highly competitive market because we're all fundamentally attracted to things that look nice. It's why we denizens of the digital world sometimes refer to things we make as 'sexy'. It may also be because we really need to get out more.

Having evolved to using graphical user interfaces, or GUIs, our first instinct was to make applications that looked like their real-world counterparts. The Apple Notebook app for example looked, well, just like a notebook, and skeuomorphism was the name of the game. Tab folders were a pretty good likeness for their paper and binder equivalents, and a button had a three-dimensional appearance and when clicked would appear to go up and down just like its namesake.

Today there are no rules as such, but the simpler and more consistent the better. Provided everything lines up properly, spacing follows an understandable convention and you haven't tried to fit everything into one little spot, you'll probably be okay. And stick with a mainstream font. There are many to choose from, and provided you don't choose one that's 'out there' it will all look just fine.

But please, don't use this one!

Comic Sans!

Those who've read *Doing IT For Money* will know my opinion on this. And those who have not can probably guess.

Some things survive the test of time and become loved as a classic. Comic Sans will not be one of them – I hope.

Overall, keep it simple, less is more and so on.

> **Top SaaS tip: The more mainstream the product, the more important the aesthetic.**

Usability

When you and the team are considering how an application will work, and how a user will navigate around it, there are a million things to consider, and it's far too big a subject to be dealt with here. However, what you should try to get to grips with is that the nature of the application is critical.

Mass market platforms tend to be comparatively simple. There are several reasons for this, not least of which is that it's aimed at the average user, and as you'll soon discover, Mr and Mrs Average User are decidedly less talented and insightful than one would hope. They're also not about to do a training course, read much by way of documentation or do anything else that might be helpful to their cause, let alone yours.

In fact, they'll expect it to 'just work', whatever that means.

However, if you're building a solution for a vertical market, and especially business users, you can build something far more complex. Businesses attach a much greater value to such products, so they tend to invest time and energy in ensuring they get the best out of their investment. This means you can get away with having far less bling. In fact, quite a few world-leading platforms are what a child of the modern era might refer to as eye-bleedingly ugly. I know I do from time to time. The focus has clearly been on delivering function rather than form, and it's still possible today to pay scant regard to the aesthetic for this market, provided your product delivers good value.

But while that remains true for some market leaders, the pressure is on. The competition is growing both bigger and up, and big markets lead to big investments. The new kids look just the way one would expect a modern application to look and they'll soon work just as well as the old ones.

Like building a house

One of my pet peeves with SaaS entrepreneurs is that so many become caught up in the aesthetic and design, but this is putting the cart before the horse. And while it's kinda fun to dream, it's a bit of a waste of time. Understanding the structural requirements, the data and functional needs is a far more important activity. This is not to say you shouldn't consider the aesthetic, merely that anything other than a very high-level view is a confusion in the early stages.

The analogy I use is that of designing a home for yourself. You might, for example, want an apex roof, a veranda out the front, clothes-line out the back, and an old rocking chair. This will help you come up with a picture and overall design. But practicality must prevail. So there's the question of how many bedrooms you want, bathrooms, living areas, garage size and flow through the home.

The colour you ultimately paint your bedroom walls is likely to be unimportant at this stage, and similarly, when you get around to building the home, wiring, plumbing and other infrastructure needs are dealt with long before anyone picks up a paintbrush.

And just like building a house, you may well get to see the framework first. In the IT world it's often referred to as 'wireframing', and it's a technique used to show how an application will fit together. The output is typically rather simplistic, but wireframes are pretty quick to build and they'll give you a good sense of what you're getting.

Keep it simple … ish … or not

In my experience, there are few if any rules that absolutely *must* be followed when designing a user interface. The word 'intuitive' seems to pop up a lot, but what that means is entirely unclear and will depend on the type of application and its needs. That said, there are lots of common patterns, and it's worthy of note that if you're heading towards a mass market, being different and out there with your design is likely a suboptimal choice.

Practically speaking, unless you're making something with limited functionality, the user interface will likely be quite complex. It's easy to get stuck on the idea of trying to make it idiot proof, but that's a largely nonsense notion driven by the many $5 apps available for your mobile. Real-world platforms that address business needs are often necessarily complicated because the data and functionality they deliver is similarly so.

It's far more important therefore that you're consistent in your approach. As users navigate around an application, the layout, size, positioning and vernacular should all follow the same rules. Once your users have learned to use one area, using another is far less challenging. After all, graphic designers will tell you to use a limited colour palette, so why not apply the same idea to functional requirements?

As the old wisdom goes, if you give a man a fish you feed him for a day. Teach him to fish and you feed him for ever. This is the same idea. Teach them the rules and they'll be good to go. And if you follow similar constructs to everyone else, educating your users will be so much easier.

> Top SaaS tip: Users don't like surprises.

Innovation ain't all that

There is one rule that you should perhaps follow though, and it's what I refer to as the 'minnow vs the whale' rule.

Apple, Microsoft and Google are the whales, and they can set their own user interface rules. An example of this is Apple's introduction of swiping from the right to delete something. Prior to its arrival, we'd all been quite happy selecting items in a list and hitting the delete button or similar. I remember seeing it for the first time and wondering how I was supposed to know to do that without someone telling me.

Still, if you're Apple with hundreds of millions of customers or so, you can innovate and the crowd will follow, begrudgingly or not.

You on the other hand are a minnow. Innovative user interface tricks will earn you more enemies than friends. So, if in doubt, indulge yourself and spend a lazy afternoon plagiarising everyone else's ideas and design something that's reassuringly just like everyone else.

Trust me when I tell you that software that's repetitive, predictable and boring as batshit is just how it should be, especially in the business space.

> **Top SaaS tip: When in Rome, do as the Romans do.**

The 'ignorable zones'

My last word on interface design is that users come with all manner of different skill levels. Happily, most are far more capable and familiar with technology than they were when I started out. Annoyingly though, there are still those who find using software difficult, and you're about to discover that you can't please all the people all the time and that some of them are very vocal about their dislike of what you've done … and maybe even you personally.

It'll sting at first, but you'll soon toughen up. After a while, you'll ignore them in the same way you do other people's crying babies … which seems to be an all too appropriate metaphor now that I've written it.

The best news is that the shouty ones tend to exist at either end of the distribution curve, in what I like to think of as the 'ignorable zones'. They tend to be the ones either pushing the envelope or struggling to tie their shoelaces, so aim squarely for the big fat bit in the middle and you should be okay.

Yet another cautionary tale

Humans, being the emotionally driven creatures that we are, sometimes let our enthusiasm get the better of us, and in the software world that can be devastating. At this point, I'll introduce you to Jerry (not his real name).

I met Jerry a few years ago. He's a delightful man. He's clever, very experienced in his field, capable, very passionate about a particular subject matter and he isn't the least bit knowledgeable about software. He did have an idea though and he wrote it down in very loose terms on one of those fag packets I mentioned earlier. Then he paid the cheapest people he could find to try to turn it into reality, and of course, they made precisely what he told them he wanted.

The result was all too predictable. The design evolved as they went along, so they spent many months rewriting and adjusting their work. Then they realised they'd never even considered how some rather important features would integrate with what they'd created, so there was yet more adjustment to be done. After twelve months of work, they had what they thought was an MVP.

This was the version I got to see, and it was painful. There were bugs aplenty, inconsistencies everywhere, and so much of what I consider the basics were just not there, including a means by which to monetise it. It was, to quote the irascible Malcolm Tucker in *The Thick of It*, ' ... a fucking omnishambles', and an eye-wateringly expensive omnishambles at that.

It never became a live product.

THE APPLICATION

Hopefully by now you're beginning to get to grips with the wonderful world that is software development. As I said before, it's no place for tourists, but when you get to the end, like climbing a big mountain, the view from the top is spectacular.

Having taken you through some of the myriad complexities of picking a development team, specifications and more, it's time for you to learn a little about the whys and wherefores of software application design and implementation, and some of the less tangible wrongs and rights.

I'll start with clearing up one of those common misconceptions.

'Hey, let's build an app ... '

As part of your design and specification process, you're going to have to make a choice about how the solution is going to be delivered to your (hopefully) many users. Your specification, design and development process will be affected by this, as will your budget, so making the right choice is rather important. Your development partner should guide you in the right direction, but just in case you've managed to pick one with a less than accurate moral compass, I'll give a couple of pointers.

For simplicity, I'll split modern applications into three groups: desktop, mobile and browser.

Desktop

These are the applications you run on your desktop or laptop, such as Word, Excel and Skype. If this is your focus, you have some very specialised processing to do that requires a massive amount of processor resources and likely some kick-ass graphics. Only a fraction of new application development targets this area, so I'm mentioning them for completeness and moving on.

Mobile

This is where the misconception comes in. Many people think they want to build an app to be downloaded from an app store directly on to a phone or tablet. But, as a general rule, they almost certainly don't.

Apps became enormously popular with the rise of smartphones, a term we used before we just called them phones because nearly all phones are now smart. Every man and his dog was getting on the bandwagon with the hope of mass market penetration and millions of downloads for a few bucks a pop. They created a version of the app for Apple and another for Android, paid both a hefty percentage for the privilege, and that was that.

And then some discovered they wanted to run the same thing in a browser on a laptop as well, so they'd have to make another version. Making three variants may not treble your costs, but doubling isn't out of the question.

There's still value in the mobile version of course, but unless you need access to specific device features like accelerometers and the like, and most business-related applications don't, you might just as well create something that runs in a browser. Then it can run anywhere you can put a browser, and today, that's just about everywhere.

Browser

Remember we're in the middle of tech revolution. We've never done this before, so we're all learning as we go. And this means there's been a few quiet little battles going on for the hearts and minds of millions of device users. One of those was between installed applications – desktop and mobile – and browser applications.

Spoiler alert: the browser won.

It is now the ubiquitous technology of choice for, well, just about everything. What used to be a means of delivering read-only pages of text and images is now the de facto choice of champions for highly functional and graphically gorgeous applications. It's only taken twenty years or so, but the IT industry has settled on an answer and we're all heading in much the same direction.

The browser became the dominant technology primarily because it offered a solution for all uses, be that a PC, a mobile device or even a fridge. Importantly, it was also able to evolve, allowing those delivering software to deploy new functionality as the technological capabilities themselves improved. What started as dumb images and text soon became highly functional and then highly graphical, and now everyone is using the same piece of software that caters for the overwhelming majority of requirements.

An all but unified IT world?! I swear I thought it would never happen, but here we are. It's almost enough to bring a tear to this cynical old pro's eye.

You can even make what's referred to as a 'progressive web app', or PWA, which can be installed on a mobile device directly from your own website without having to pay a third party for the pleasure.

Take that Apple and Google!

So, to sum up. You're almost certainly going to build a browser application.

Developing for different devices

That your application will run in a browser presents developers with a challenge. I'm currently writing this in Word on a laptop attached to a 27-inch monitor with a 1920 × 1080 resolution. If I look at a website or application, it's formatted accordingly. On a different device – my iPhone 13 Pro Max, for instance – there's simply not enough room to show the same information in the same manner. Browsers detect this difference and use instructions buried in the code for the page to show the content appropriately.

Developers need to make these choices and it's referred to as 'responsive design'. A browser simply isn't clever enough to do this on its own. Simple cases can be managed by flowing screen artefacts down the page, but that's about it. In reality, decisions for many things have to be made on a case-by-case basis.

If that's not enough to be going on with, there's also a marked difference between how we use a device with a mouse and with a finger. The former is very precise while the latter, if my own digital dexterity is anything to go by, is most certainly not. There are differences too between how we interact with a device. Point and click and touch, while similar, are far from identical. For example, we can move a mouse over something and hover. After a brief wait we might see a hint or additional information. If you hover your finger over something on a phone, you're going to be disappointed.

And try swiping left or right with a mouse on your laptop.

Lastly, screen sizes are becoming bigger. 4K screens are now becoming popular with 3840 × 2160 pixels, and if that's not enough, 8K is four times larger still at 7680 × 4320. Imagine if you designed something for a phone and then ran it on a 100-inch screen at that resolution. There's going to be a lot of dead space.

Choosing your target

Given the variety of targets, it's wise to settle on two or three core sizes. Perhaps consider small, medium and large variants. Small is for phones and designed for touch, which requires more space between screen elements. Medium is for tablets and also designed for touch, but with more available screen space so you can show more data. Large is for laptops and bigger screens but designed for a mouse and point and click.

It may be however that your application is suitably complex that it would make no sense to try to use it on a mobile phone. If this is the case you can simply design for a larger size and leave it at that. When it runs on the phone it will look like a rather cramped small version of the big one. It will still work, but it won't be overly usable, and that's okay.

Remember, you're building a tool to solve someone's problem. Just as you pick a niche to give you more focus in terms of selling and messaging, your application benefits from precisely the same rationale. It doesn't have to be all things to all people in all circumstances.

Top SaaS tip: You're selling to somebody, not everybody.

One size does not fit all

One size might be suitable for all, and it may even deliver an outcome for everyone, but does it truly fit?

We know of course that it doesn't. I'm sure you've bought clothes before that just weren't right. They'd obviously been made to a price and were therefore cut accordingly. No big deal with a T-shirt, but there are better examples of the 'flaw of averages'.

Take the American Airforce, for example. They tried to build an average cockpit for their pilots in the 1950s. They measured several thousand men and started working out the averages for neck size, thigh circumference, waist and so on. What they found was that none of the pilots was average.

This might sound a little odd at first but think about it for a moment. For simplicity, imagine you have an equal distribution of five assorted sizes for each of these three metrics. Pick a person at random and he has a 1 in 125 chance of being the same as another random selection. And that's only using three variables.

Mass market platforms solve this issue by not caring one jot about the needs of an individual, instead assuming it's pretty much a numbers game and as long as they find enough people, they'll have plenty of revenue. It's why we're all treated so woefully by telecom providers and power companies.

But if we're building a more focused solution, let's say a project management SaaS platform, and there are literally hundreds of those, fit becomes an important notion for the simple reason that not all users are the same. Each will have their own needs, and while they may need access to the same information, they may not want to see it in the same format. For example, a manager looking at the work being done by the team will want to see everyone, while the individual will only be interested in their own to-do list.

Idiot to expert

Users come in many forms and with varying skill levels and domain knowledge. To help us understand the many differing needs a platform will face, we typically create what are referred to as 'user personas', and as you've probably already realised, for any given platform there can be quite a few of those.

This is especially true for products with a specific focus. Mass market offerings will likely only have a handful, perhaps three or four. Vertical market and service SaaS platforms may have many, and the needs and wants of each group will be markedly different. For example, the team in the office managing incoming orders will have a vastly different set of needs to the picking team in the warehouse.

Most importantly, they may have quite different skill levels too, and it's this that can have the most profound effect on your solution. Mass market products typically assume users have minimal skill, and as you can't send them all on a training course, the interface is kept very simple. Data is kept to a minimum, spacing is bigger and it takes more clicks and navigation to get things done.

Conversely, on niche platforms, users are more likely to be experts with a far greater understanding of the domain. Notably, they're often a captive audience and training will likely be a part of implementation. This means the UI can be far more complex with a busier interface and more data on the screen.

When you're considering the designs for your various screens, I suggest strongly that you make sure you're engaging a design professional and not just a programmer as part of the process. They'll be able to guide you in the right direction and it will make a massive difference to the overall result.

Top SaaS tip: Not all data is equally important.

SUMMARY

Prior preparation does indeed prevent poor performance, and if it doesn't, it does at least give you a fighting chance. But perfection is the enemy of done, and if you're planning on world domination it's best to get to market. So how do you know when you've spent enough time preparing and you're ready to start building?

You'll know.

You'll have spent countless hours going round and round making sure that the data model looks like it should work. You'll have seen numerous wireframes and sketches that seem to look pretty good and you'll have come up with a big pile of business rules.

Building a software platform demands that you dissect everything you know and then put it back together in a far more structured and organised way. So the time you spend planning will be highly educational, and it will teach you a great deal about your world. Once you think you've got it down pat, it's time to start turning it into reality.

This is where the fun and frustration really start.

Top SaaS tip: If you're not a little scared, you probably haven't understood what's coming.

CHAPTER 5

BUILD

By now you'll feel like your plans are ready to be put into action, the team will be revved up and raring to go, and your cash will be burning a hole in your pocket. But a word of caution, no battle plan survives first contact with the enemy, and software development teaches humility very quickly. Your seemingly simple project is going to be far more annoying than you could possibly have imagined.

Still, such is life. If you're brave enough or mad enough, and there's a fine line between the two, to get involved in the murky world of commercial software, frustration is just another part of life's rich pageant and you're going to have to learn to live with it.

The best way to deal with this, in my opinion, is to put your grownup boots on and to wade right on in. So, let's get on with it, and this is your next target.

MINIMUM VIABLE PRODUCT

All that time and effort writing a spec was undoubtedly a big job, and it's important to get as much included as possible because it provides a long-term target to aim at. However, your software will never be finished. You'll be adding to it for years to come, so a pragmatic approach is required if you're going to get to market and start making a dollar or two.

This means you need to build an MVP, or minimum viable product. However, quite what constitutes an MVP is unclear, and the decisions that drive what gets included will vary greatly depending on your circumstances and, for that matter, who you ask.

My definition

Here's my take on what an MVP should be, and the clue is in the name.

Minimum – The least.

Viable – That works.

Product – That delivers value.

So, an MVP as far as I'm concerned is a version of your software that's the least that works and delivers value.

So far so good, but if you cast your mind back to the beginning, I said that we create software to solve someone's problem, so that begs the question as to whose problem we're solving. To understand that we need to know why we have created our product.

Why build an MVP?

There are two primary drivers for creating your MVP: knowledge and money.

We're interested in the former because we need to know whether we're heading in roughly the right direction. Many SaaS ventures fail simply because their idea doesn't have a market, or they're targeting the wrong one. Building a bare bones version allows you to test the waters a little and to get your idea in front of a few potential punters to see what they think.

So, before we throw huge piles of cash into our potential SaaS money pit, we invest a relatively small amount and get an early version out there. That way we can get some feedback and work out whether we're metaphorically hitting the nail on the head, or if we're perhaps a little wide of the mark and our thumb has bravely taken one for the team.

The second reason is of course cash, because most start-ups have limited funds and exist on the smell of an oily rag, pizza and Coke.

That uppercase C is really important, don't you think?

So, the quicker a meaningful example can be constructed, the less it costs to make and the sooner it can be presented to investors and early adopters in the hope they might get on board and join in the fun.

So an MVP exists to solve your problems as well as your clients', and is really just a tactical position you take on your journey towards your strategic goal. It's a line in the development sand from which you can gain a whole heap of insights and hopefully some cold hard cash as well. And if you're smart, it will help you sharpen your development efforts, allowing you to better organise your priorities.

Seven principles for creating a successful MVP

That's the theory, but what does it mean with regards to your project?

The answer is of course that it depends, but perhaps the most important consideration is that your MVP is not the final answer. It's a base on which you can build, or should you find yourself somewhat in the mire, it's a place from which you can still make a tactical retreat, regroup and reassess your options.

Either way, trying to determine what's wrong or right is as ever a little tricky, so to guide your thinking, here are a few basic principles. And remember, you're building the least that works and delivers value …

- **Don't sweat the tech.** Unless you have some very specific needs, the choice of tools, language, database and so on really doesn't matter that much. So, think bare bones, keep it simple and get the job done.

- **Go end to end.** Make sure the user can get from a reasonable beginning to a result so they can see the value you deliver. Potential for success is nowhere near as valuable as success itself, which is why all cricket captains will tell you it's better to have runs on the board than wickets in hand.

- **Focus on your core.** Your MVP is here to prove a point, so forget bells and whistles because they're a distraction. All they do is encourage your users to look at something other than your core value.

- **Smoke and mirrors are good.** You're not looking for perfection. If there are a few hacks or manual interventions along the way, so what? These are just features you're yet to fully implement or automate. Remember, knowledge or money.

- **Look and feel ain't all that.** Don't waste time making things pretty. As long as it looks professional and competent, you're ready to go. The user interface is guaranteed to change as you learn and build more.

- **Don't reinvent the wheel.** Remember, you're not showing off your technical prowess. If someone else has already solved a problem for you, it makes sense to leverage their work. So, where you can, integrate with and use third-party offerings to get across the line. They might not be perfect, but they'll do for today and you can always change them tomorrow.

And lastly, and probably most importantly …

- **Get to market.** Seriously – *get to [expletive] market!* You can spend years perfecting an MVP, but what's the point? Get it out there, warts and all. Because in my experience, the first 20% of a platform delivers 80% of the value. And that will likely be all that your prospects will ever need to see.

Brave Sir Robin ran away

There is a distinct possibility your MVP will turn out not to be fit for purpose and as such it will have zero commercial value. If it does, you're certainly not the first and you most definitely won't be the last. Should this rather disappointing scenario eventuate, you have but one question to answer. Should I continue?

The answer of course is it depends. Some situations are salvageable, and with a little realignment and hard work, it's entirely possible that your MVP or early versions can be turned into something else. Instagram is an excellent example of this. It started life as Burbn, an app for checking in to hotels. However, its founders realised it was rather similar to another app and so they shifted their focus to their photo sharing feature that was popular with early adopters.

The rest as they say is history.

Sometimes it's the technology that holds you back. I encountered this in the early days of Visual LANSA Web when we tried to convert some existing code as a shortcut. The team got it to work, but the result was simply too big to be a viable solution. I still recall the meeting where the boss asked if we were going to carry on, and I remember telling him that it was time to be grownups and we had to call it a day with that technique. Four months of work down the drain in little more than five minutes.

Happily, one of my colleagues had been telling us all along that he knew the right way to do it. And he did, too. So we went back to work, salvaging what we could.

However, while these are two shiny examples of what can happen, by now you should be well aware that these are the exceptions rather than the rule. Most of the time, failed MVPs are nothing more than a bigger failure waiting to happen.

If all of the soon-to-be failed SaaS wannabes I've ever encountered had given me 20% of their investment and shut up shop as I'd suggested, I'd be a heap richer and they'd still have 80% of their money. But where's the fun in that? If we don't dream, try, fail and learn, we never grow. There's value aplenty to be found in the process of failing, and who knows, perhaps a first-time disaster is precisely the education one needs so they can smash it out of the park next time around.

As Reg says in *Life of Brian*, 'Siblings! Let us not be downhearted. One total catastrophe like this is just the beginning!', and while that's a little tongue in cheek, it's often said that investors in the US prefer an entrepreneur with a couple of bankruptcies under their belt.

But if that's not for you, bravely running away is nothing to be ashamed of. No one sane will ever criticise you for deciding not to gamble a big pile of cash.

THE DEVELOPMENT PROCESS

Once you have a team and you know what's going to be included in your MVP, you can sit back and let the gang get on with it. All you have to do is supply some cash periodically and that's that.

Ahh … if only it were that simple.

You're about to discover that the development process requires a little more input than that.

The problem is that your developers are unlikely to know what you know. Yes, there's a spec and that will get them a long way, but there's always some domain knowledge and nuance only an expert will really understand. Your guys will be able to create the database and start building out much of the functionality, but they're going to need your help to deliver that certain je ne sais quoi.

Don't be shy

You might not be overly savvy when it comes to software design and programming, but that doesn't mean your opinion is irrelevant. Remember, you're the first person to see what they're making and your opinion will likely reflect that of your customers. And in case you'd forgotten, your financial future and/or professional career may be on the line. This means it's in your best interests to ask a stack of questions about the dumbest of things.

This can be hard for a lot of people. Being seen to be ignorant, confrontational or challenging about an unfamiliar subject doesn't sit comfortably with many, and we have a tendency to sit quietly and let the grownups talk. I do this when my wife is arranging our finances. It's a subject I don't really get, and they use a funny language I don't properly understand.

So kinda like a lot of IT people talking then.

Ahh, hoisted by my own petard. Bugger.

Still, as unpleasant as it may be, it's best that you swallow any lingering vestiges of pride and just get on with it. You'll feel like a chump at first and they may well find your questions funny and laugh at you behind your back, or even to your face, but so what? You've a load of cash and reputation on the line and looking a bit of a moron for a while is a small price to pay.

Besides, the more you engage, the more you'll learn, the more you'll be able to converse with the team and the better you'll all understand each other.

Trust me on this on. I've spent my career asking the dumbest of questions and occasionally wondering, and probably along with those in the room with me, whether I was in the right place.

The Pareto principle

Nothing quite prepares you for the first time you see your working platform, even if it's at its most simple and barely more than a wire-frame. You may even get to see something working within the first few days. But be warned, the eighty-twenty rule is here to make sure you keep your feet firmly on the ground.

When it comes to software, the devil is very much in the detail, and while you might be able to see a screen, it doesn't mean that it's real and delivering value. It may well be little more than smoke and mirrors. This is one of the harsh realities of product development. The first 20% of the work may look like it's delivered 80% of the desired outcome, but it hasn't. It just happens to have created some of the visible bits.

I remember showing the boss an early proof of concept version of Visual LANSA Web. It was built on top of the existing platform, so it looked robust and almost complete, but we'd only done about 5% of the development work. It took another eighteen months to get anything remotely resembling a complete product.

Developer productivity

Software development is without doubt one of the most frustrating activities to engage in, especially for those paying for the pleasure. It is, to quote a SaaS CEO that I know, 'eye-bleedingly slow at times'.

Much has been written about productivity, particularly with regards to the specifics of the development process, but these tend to be rather low level, nuts and bolts ideas, such as avoiding distractions and using code snippets. While these are all clearly important, they're really something that your team should be able to manage comfortably. I'd like you to look at the problem from a slightly higher vantage point.

For me, developer productivity is divided into three areas.

Team

Despite the appearance of software being developed by lots of people in their own little bubbles, reality is far from that. Development is a team game, and the bigger the platform gets, the more important it is to have a coherent, professionally managed group.

Regular and effective communication is essential, from both a project management and leadership perspective. Developers need a coherent target to aim at and a consistent vision. Your job is to ensure such things exist. If you don't know where the business is going, you can't expect your team to follow.

Tools

'Is there something free we can use?'

I was asked that once by an entrepreneur hoping to cut a corner or two and save a dollar in the process. Our relationship was such that I couldn't be quite as honest as I'd have liked, so I politely suggested that such ideas were often false economies.

Expensive development tools are just commercial software, so the same principles you're applying to determine value for your platform will apply to them just as much. They may seem expensive, but given the cost of a developer, they represent excellent value.

Also, developers can often be attracted to the next shiny thing, and it's all too easy to wind up with a 'one of everything' problem, where every time a new problem comes up, a new tool is used to solve it. But, if you're clear about what you're building you can determine nearly all of your tool needs up front.

Processes and practices

There are numerous shortcuts and hacks that developers can use to help them write code, but only a fraction of what they do requires them to press buttons on the keyboard. So, whether you're using agile, waterfall, a mixture of both, something else, or a new technique that's just been invented, development efficiency is all about implementation.

All tasks need to be turned into manageable pieces and their place in the process well understood. If you have a big job that may take many weeks, break it down into smaller pieces. Quite what makes something the right size is entirely personal, and it doesn't help that some tasks must be completed before others can start while others need to be done contemporaneously.

There's also a balance to be struck between checking each decision as you go along and giving your team the freedom to keep moving. If, for example, you need a design to be checked before coding can start, you're guaranteeing that a developer will jump on to the next job or just sit around waiting. Clearly this is not a good situation and transfer costs from task switching are horrific. Experience has shown me that while one task might take an hour from end to end, two one-hour tasks will take three, and three one-hour jobs can take eight. Allowing developers to focus on a single topic then will save you countless hours.

However, too little oversight and you risk a lot of expensive refactoring and rewriting, something typically best avoided, but regrettably necessary sometimes to ensure a focus on quality. As ever then, a pragmatic position that allows developers to keep moving with just enough peer review and control is the sweet spot. Clearly that's something that will be specific to your organisation and your project, and there is no definitive arrangement. Best then is to engage with your team and find out what's working and what isn't.

Measuring

Whatever you do, you'll need to decide on and record metrics about your team's performance. This might be the number of defects created, lines of code written, tasks completed and more. (There are many things you can record, and there's a section that explores this in detail in chapter seven on ownership.)

Most important is that you don't compare yourself with others too harshly. There are many opinions as to what's good and bad, but for me this is all about individual performance and how you're doing today compared to yesterday. If your metrics are improving, that's enough. There are far too many variables for a simple side-by-side comparison with your peers to be of much value.

Utilisation and capacity

Software development is sometimes considered to be a form of manufacturing. That being the case, you might think that ideas like Goldratt's Theory of Constraints and Drum Buffer Rope apply, and to some extent they do.

However, while there are many similarities, particularly with regards to ideas around resolving limiting factors and removing bottlenecks, there is a major difference. Manufacturing repeats defined activities with known times. Software development is a little more of an artform, with estimates for completion typically being out by at least 50%. Further to this, humans are nowhere near as good as machines at switching task, with a context switch typically taking about half an hour or so.

It's important then not to overload the team and to remember they're human. I tend to think of a football team trying to score. Only a few players will be running at any moment. Some will be gently trotting into position and others will be waiting for their moment of glory. If they all work together, the team is efficient, effective, and scores.

Forcing them all to keep running all the time simply doesn't work. The right people won't be in the right place at the right time.

Top SaaS tip: Nine women can't make a baby in a month.

A quick aside about programmers

You'll likely have limited interaction with the button-pressing people at the sharp end until you've built your own team. Instead, you'll probably deal with a project manager of some sort. They're generally quite normal and quite capable of talking like typical human beings.

Happy days!

But, you might just have to interact with some developers, and while obviously most of them are not stereotypical geeky nerds lacking in empathy, social skills and access to sunlight, some of them most assuredly are.

They're easy to spot though. Their keyboards only have three buttons – zero, one and enter.

You know, because real programmers code in binary.

It's a computer gag.

I'm not going to apologise for it. I told you at the start I've got very little to work with here.

A former programmer colleague, and highly functional human, told me of a time when he joined a large business. On his second day he introduced himself to one of his new teammates and asked if he had a few moments to show him what he was doing and talk him through his new environment. Normal people would of course say something like, 'Sure. No problem. Pleased to meet you,' and so on.

Instead, all he got was a blank face, a dull-eyed stare and a rather abrupt, 'No'.

The individual concerned is now referred to by an appropriate moniker, but decorum prevents me from sharing it here.

However, this somewhat dystopian and anachronistic view of programmers is some way from reality. My recent work in enterprise meant I was lucky enough to meet a great many young developers fresh from university. A few have rather a lot of 'me' work to do, but most are just very bright girls and guys who happen to like technology, and they'll be all the better at it tomorrow if we all make the effort to engage with them should the chance arise.

Empathy might not be their strongest suit, but I promise, they're nothing to fear. You might even learn something from them.

I know I did.

None of us is as dumb as all of us

When you do get to chat with your project team, and perhaps some developers, it's all too easy to get lost in both the detail and translation, the latter of which is nothing more than an occupational hazard. It's why it's so important that you make the effort to learn as much as you can about the software world, and precisely why I'm writing this book.

Ultimately, trusting your development team to get it right is the way to go, but they will need guidance, and at times you will disagree.

And then you'll compromise.

And sometimes, none of you will feel comfortable with the answer.

This is the 'none of us is as dumb as all of us' moment, and it's not just a computing thing. It happens in many walks of life when opinionated humans gather to determine a best path forward.

You need to learn to recognise it and call it out in the moment. It can have painful consequences that cost a lot of time and money to fix. I'd love to give you a specific example here, but the many I have to choose from are all too complex to explain. Suffice to say, I've spent many, many hours undoing stupid decisions resulting from meetings where I was neither brave enough nor smart enough to put a stop to what later became the blindingly obvious.

Happily, I've now developed a couple of techniques to help avoid these situations:

- Limit the number of people in a meeting. Once you get above four or perhaps five, it's all too easy to become caught up in groupthink as you search for a consensus.

- When you're stuck, put it in the too-hard basket and come back to it. Finding the right answer can be awfully difficult. Spotting a wrong answer though is less so. So rather than accepting a compromise, simply accept you don't know what to do and ignore it for now. Then you can take it easy. Let your mind wander and the creative juices work their magic, and you may well find you come up with a better answer later.

  Of course, that too may not be the right answer and you get to go round again … and again … and again, depending on how muscular your OCD is. Mine used to take steroids and do some serious weight training.

Round and round and round

Software development is an iterative process. Unlike physical engineering, where precise plans can be defined and then implemented with relatively few changes, in the software world there are simply far too many small things to get right up front. This is not to say that you can't get a great deal organised before you start, and your spec will help greatly here, but the best you can do is break the process down into smallish bits with some basic instructions as to what happens within each.

This is essentially the traditional waterfall approach to software development, and if I'm honest for day-to-day application development it's a perfectly reasonable technique that does its best to make sure everything is shipshape and Bristol fashion.

And then there's agile, and if ever there's a word that's been overused, this is it. The original agile manifesto was a set of twelve principles that are all very sensible, and I thoroughly recommend you look them up. A simple search on Google for 'agile manifesto' will find them soon enough.

Development teams and developers can get a little dogmatic about these things though, and like any tool, its efficacy will depend more on the people using it than the tool itself. Agile is very much the popular choice today and it represents a very fluid and largely pragmatic approach. So I'll reprise what I wrote in *Doing IT For Money* and tell you I'm a fan of neither ignorance nor dogma. I prefer to know as much up front as possible and to be able to adjust course as I'm going along.

Top SaaS tip: Create a solid plan, follow it and deal with the unexpected as necessary.

Seven ways to waste development dollars

What I've always found most frustrating about the development process is that the first few weeks and sometimes months can be spent building infrastructure, so there's nothing much to see beyond some very simple mock-ups. It's even more frustrating for the uninitiated. I've had numerous meetings over the years where I've had to appease senior leaders whose expectations had little to do with reality.

Imagine how it's going to feel when it's your money being spent and you've got little to show for it. Now imagine how that might feel if you have the same experience but you've run out of money.

I've seen it firsthand and it's heartbreaking. It was one of the drivers for me to write this book. So, with that in mind, here are a few ways for you to haemorrhage cash. Avoid these, and you'll be far more likely to keep your eyes on the prize and get the biggest and best bang for your buck:

- **Building the wrong thing.** Unless you're focused on specific customer needs, it's all too easy to build features and other stuff that won't be used. So, stick to your spec and the plan, unless you absolutely must make changes.

- **Lacking focus.** As I wrote just a few pages ago, context switching is a killer, and the more jobs a developer has on the go the longer each will take to do. Worse is that it can become the accepted norm, so rather than sticking to one thing at a time complication becomes standard practice.

- **Over complication.** Yes, I know you want your platform to do *everything*, and one day it will. But right now, it needs to do enough, and that's all. So keep it simple.

- **Poor communication.** Confusion and chaos always come with a big cost, so be absolutely clear in all that you say and do. As I said before, don't be shy in coming forward and asking questions.

- **Doing the wrong work.** Developers are funny things. Occasionally, they like to do a little bit more, because, you know, it's fun and kinda helpful and … yeah. The trouble is, you're paying, so it's incumbent on you to make sure they're following the spec to the letter. It's why you agreed on it in the first place.

  Your project manager should be on top of this, but it's always good to have another pair of eyes.

- **Requiring rework.** Some rework is inevitable. It's one of those occupational hazard things and part of the development experience. It usually comes about because humans are involved and they're horribly imperfect. That's the nice version. It sometimes comes about because they're just not that good at the job.

- **Using somebody else's code.** If there's one thing developers dislike, it's someone else's code. It's a language, and just as two people will use different words and grammar to describe something, so it is with the code they write. If developers have to tackle other people's spaghetti, it can take them a long time to work out how it all hangs together. It's why having a decent-sized team behind you can make all the difference.

Getting on with it

I could probably write another book about the development process alone. It is an extraordinarily complex world full of subtlety, nuance, dogma, opinion and so much more, but I'm going to move on to the remainder of this tome. There's so much more to cover and you really don't need to be overly involved in the minutiae of programming.

Once you're engaging regularly with the team, providing feedback, assisting where you can, looking at what's being produced and so on, there's not a whole heap more you can do. And it's not as if there isn't a great deal more for you to be thinking about. Going to market will be front and centre all too soon and there'll be plenty of prep work for you to do.

Still, before you get too far into the build of your application, there are a few other subjects worthy of a quick mention.

SPEED AND QUALITY

There is an ongoing battle in the minds of many in the software development family between speed of development and quality of product.

The argument goes like this.

Complete software is the only practical measure of success, so getting your platform built and to market is the goal. To achieve this, it may be necessary to focus less on iterating to achieve the best quality and more on getting the job done. Any bugs created as a by-product are just a cost of doing business and can be dealt with after release.

The counter argument says that quality must be the focus. Mistakes now will be far more expensive to remedy later, and a poor customer experience could lead to a loss of revenue and reputation. Better then to take the time to find the right answer rather than the first and to keep going until the product is ready to face the enemy.

The perception is that quality and speed exist as two sides in a zero-sum game. Increase one and the other will decrease, and vice versa.

Building on sand

This idea sounds true, but the software world is far more nuanced, and it rides roughshod over such simple mantras. For example, if you were to tell the team that there are no time constraints, would they make a perfect solution? The answer clearly is no. Mistakes are inevitable because humans are involved and there is a low watermark beyond which the cost of finding one's mistakes becomes too high.

When it comes to speed, we might think of the early days of Facebook and the oft cited aphorism of 'move fast and break things'. This might suggest that development speed is everything, and who are we to argue with Zuckerberg? But it was really a reference to management processes and internal structure more than coding and the platform itself.

Agility and speed in the development process are important, and getting to market is the ultimate goal, but there's little point in shooting yourself in the foot. Building a platform that requires a lot of rework later is a false economy. It's why developers will tell you to never code around a mistake. Fix the problem, and it will likely remain fixed forever.

Taking the time to invest in quality and to create a solid foundation is therefore crucial to your long-term prospects, and as I'll keep saying, success in SaaS comes when you play the long game.

Young vs old

The age of the organisation makes a significant difference here too. Young businesses simply don't have the resources to invest in building out their own systems, automation, education and much more. They're typically head down bum up getting shit done, and quality is often measured rather simplistically by the number of issues being created.

But quality is much more than that and you'll gain a far better understanding of your team's performance by estimating the number of mistakes and errors in the entirety of the development process from ideation through to delivery, the number of pairs of hands involved, the delay caused by such, and so on. If we limit ourselves to a rather blunt count of coding errors, we're somewhat missing the point.

If you're looking at the technology … something something.

Older organisations with a more mature development process have solved many of these issues because they've had the chance to invest in the many ancillary systems that mean humans are removed from the loop. As such, they have found ways to improve quality at many points in the delivery cycle. For them, it's not quality or speed but more that their quality enables speed.

I bet many are still looking at the number of bugs they have though.

INTELLECTUAL PROPERTY

Before I start on this topic, I am not a lawyer, and this is not legal advice. I strongly recommend you seek specialist software IP guidance. Right, with my rear appropriately covered, let's have a quick look at some legal things.

What is it?

Intellectual property is anything you create in your mind, so inventions, anything you think up and then write or design, images, movies, symbols and doubtless many more.

What it *isn't* is anything your customers create while they're using the software you've provided, just as this document that I'm writing in Word doesn't belong to Microsoft.

For a full explanation of IP in Australia, look up IP Australia. Our government has done a fantastic job and put everything you might want to know in one place.

Ownership

Do you own your IP?

Well, of course you do, right? Nobody can just take it. Surely no one would hire some developers, share all their industry knowledge and unique personal insights, pay them handsomely for their efforts, and then just let them run off with everything.

Nah … no one would do that.

Would they?

Hopefully you didn't, haven't, wouldn't and aren't about to.

The annoying thing about software IP is that it's very easy to steal. If you're a furniture maker, you can lock up your workshop when you go home and your work is safe enough. If you're a software creator, all a thieving employee need do is make a 'backup'.

It's rather important then that you protect this most critical of all your assets, and that has to be done through legal channels. In Australia, there are two primary considerations.

Patents

A patent gives you exclusive rights to your creation, but obtaining one is often hard, expensive and time consuming, and the requirements vary greatly depending on where you are in the world. It is an important issue though, and patents may become valuable assets. However, in the early days it's likely something you can put on the backburner.

Copyright

Copyright covers the code, screen elements, documentation and so on. Essentially, software is treated much like any other literary work.

The good news is that in Australia your creations are protected by the copyright laws the moment they are documented on paper or electronically. However, as with patents, different jurisdictions have different rules and you may need to register your copyright. This is certainly the case in the United States.

Control

While a patent, copyright and your legal rights must be considered, until you're up and running and making a few bucks, ownership isn't your biggest IP concern.

Who controls your IP is.

If you're a business leader with an inhouse team, you can probably feel confident that you're pretty much in control. They're your team, it's your stuff, and it's likely stored where you can easily get hold of it.

But if you're dealing with a third party, the situation is less clear.

Development teams go out of business from time to time. They might, as we saw in the cautionary tale about Julie, not be up to the job, or they may just lose a few key team members and your development may stall.

So, how do you keep control?

Firstly, you need access to the source code, but while this is the physical manifestation of your IP, it's not the full story. What's just as important is an understanding of how all the little bits fit together. It's a somewhat sobering notion that the knowledge locked away in the minds of your developers is almost as valuable as the code itself.

And the bigger and older the platform, the more important that becomes because you can't go out and buy it. It has to be learned.

So do what you can to protect not only the IP itself, but also its custodians. You're going to need them both tomorrow.

GOING INTERNATIONAL

As you're doubtless dreaming of world domination, you're going to have to deal with multiple languages and multiple jurisdictions. I'll write more about going international later, but it's a subject that needs to be raised quite early in the process because it can affect your development.

The good news is that making an application that supports multiple languages has never been easier. As usual, this doesn't mean that it's easy, simply that it's less difficult than it used to be.

Way back when, we had a slew of individual code pages, each of which supported a set of characters and symbols, and just for fun there were lots of different vendors, each with their own set. Each letter, number, symbol or control character had its own value, so the code page used when data was entered needed to be the same used when it was displayed again. Without this, there was a risk that data would appear corrupted, even though the stored value would be correct.

Today Unicode has unified the world. The latest version has over 140,000 different characters available, including myriad emojis.

However, what Unicode doesn't do is translate your text for you. That's something you'll have to handle as and when the time comes, and here's a top tip. Don't rely on Google Translate getting it right. It might work at a basic level, but domain-specific language is really not its forte. Add to that a lack of context because much of your text will be descriptions and labels on the screen and there's a recipe for disaster right there.

If you're never going to be international your team can hard code English text in the source code. If you are, you need the mechanisms for multiple languages built in. This will allow the text to be replaced at runtime with the right language.

Similarly, number and date formats change around the world. English-speaking countries typically use a decimal point and a comma separator; for example, 123,456.78. This is reversed in mainland Europe, where it's 123.456,78. UK English dates are shown as day then month then year: 13/01/2023. In the US, it's 01/13/2023.

Dealing with these isn't particularly difficult, but it needs to be done throughout the application. Retrofitting the necessary bits and pieces is a pain, so it's best to consider the requirement sooner rather than later.

> **Top SaaS tip: Humans aren't the fastest translators, but they are the best.**

ARTIFICIAL INTELLIGENCE

I'm sure many of you are very excited about the possibilities that AI represents, and I'm equally sure that some of you will be almost as eager as a small child on Christmas morning to start playing with the latest and greatest toys.

Perhaps then a little reality check is in order.

What is AI?

In simplistic terms, it's our best efforts at using computing technology to imitate human capabilities.

So, we're using it for speech recognition, machine vision, language processing and making expert decisions. We're also using it as a marketing gimmick, regardless of whether the features built into the product are really AI or just a clever bit of processing that makes it look cool.

For example, there are toothbrushes with 'AI'. Apparently, they detect all sorts of things to do with where you're brushing, for how long, how hard and whether you've missed a bit.

Is that clever? Absolutely.

Is it artificial intelligence? I don't know how to spell that kinda long meh sound I make when I'm trying to say 'I don't think so' without committing fully to a no, so I'll say probably not.

I'll tell you what, though. If it could inspect my teeth, spot a cavity forming, call my dentist and book a spot in my calendar, I'd agree that it is. Sadly, we're a way from that happening.

AI is nothing new, and there's a saying in the IT industry that this year's AI is next year's software. What that means is that the techniques we develop this year may seem groundbreaking, but they're just new techniques. Once we become familiar with them and once they become more mainstream, they're just another tool for us to use as we build more and more.

How does AI work?

It's clever maths and text parsing. That's pretty much it. I don't for a moment wish to belittle my brilliant colleagues in this extraordinary area, but they are bound by both their own fundamentally human capabilities and those of the computers they're using. Of course, when quantum computing becomes a thing, and it seems increasingly likely that it will, I may need to reassess this.

Still, for now, clever maths and text parsing are the state of the art.

Does it just ... work?

No, and it's incredibly flawed.

AI systems need to be trained, so they're only as good as the person doing the training, and the data on which the training is based.

This means that AI systems invariably have biases, and often these manifest themselves along racial and gender lines.

There are numerous examples of this, and once more Google will return many pages of them. Suffice to say then that as the UK data watchdog is investigating bias against people from diverse backgrounds – so, not white males – you can probably assume there's a fair amount of smoke and the discovery of fire is likely imminent.

AI also needs a lot of data, and I mean loads, and developing algorithms is incredibly complex. This is because there are many parameters, and it's why AI is still very much in its infancy and failing to really impact business and enterprise in the way which many, myself included, would like to imagine it could.

Evolution vs design

What might seem obvious to us as adult humans after billions of years of evolution can still be next to impossible for AI, at least for now, and there are a couple of classic conundrums that continue to cause us great consternation.

The trolley problem

This is an ethical dilemma first proposed by Philippa Foot.

One variant of the story has a tram charging down the track towards four people tied to the rails. Next to you is a lever that will adjust the track and change the direction of the tram, and you have just a few moments to make your decision. But just as you're about to pull the lever you see a single person tied to the second line.

With no time to spare you have but two choices.

Do you do nothing, condemning the four to a grizzly death, or pull the lever and choose to kill just one?

This is such a simple problem on the surface, but it gets very complicated very quickly and there is no right answer. You may think there is of course, and you may choose to pull the lever because one death is better than four, but would you change your mind if the one was pregnant with twins and the four were all convicted killers?

The point is that we never have enough information to make a judgement call, and even if we did, it would be *our* opinion and *our* value system, and others may well disagree with our principles. So we can thank our lucky stars that it's a hypothetical question, except that for those engaged in the development of self-driving vehicles it is most assuredly a real problem. They have to program their car to avoid a collision, but in doing so, what is acceptable for it to hit instead?

Winograd schema

This is a test of machine intelligence devised by Hector Levesque and it stems from the ambiguity that exists in spoken language. Consider this simple statement.

The father couldn't lift his son because he was too heavy.

If I ask you who 'he' refers to, you'd say the son because you immediately understand that lifting is difficult if something is heavy.

Now I'll make a simple change.

The father couldn't lift his son because he was too weak.

If I ask you who 'he' refers to now, you'd say the father because you understand that lifting is difficult if someone is weak.

One word difference and the pronoun 'he' in an otherwise identical statement now refers to a different person. We get this because we understand the context and nuance of our language and how the words that follow help clarify what came before. For computers today, this is plain difficult.

Ethical use

So, AI's not all that, and it's prone to mistakes, but it can still add great value to a platform, especially if you have a lot of data to play with.

There is an important notion for you to understand though, and it harks back to my regular comment of, if you're looking at the technology, you're missing the point.

As mentioned, AI is biased. It's also utterly uncaring. You – I hope – are not.

I was involved with some research by Flinders University in Adelaide. This was undertaken to help government ensure the right questions are asked to help businesses understand the risk of what they're getting in to. For many, the biggest risk is that they don't understand the implications of implementing AI systems.

If we use AI as part of a decision-making system and we have no human intervention in the process, we're adding significant risk to our business. Complaints are still relatively rare, but the drums are beginning to beat louder. It's surely only a matter of time before there's a class action against someone, and when it comes it will set a precedent.

Governments the world over are beginning to recognise this and they're developing frameworks to help businesses find the right way forward. I was part of the Australian effort. After roundtables around the country, including business, academia and government, we came up with the following principles. (Search for 'Australia's Artificial Intelligence Ethics Framework' and you'll find a great deal more information courtesy of the Federal Government.)

- **Human, societal and environmental wellbeing.** AI systems should benefit individuals, society and the environment.

- **Human-centred values.** AI systems should respect human rights, diversity, and the autonomy of individuals.

- **Fairness.** AI systems should be inclusive and accessible and should not involve or result in unfair discrimination against individuals, communities or groups.

- **Privacy protection and security.** AI systems should respect and uphold privacy rights and data protection and ensure the security of data.

- **Reliability and safety.** AI systems should reliably operate in accordance with their intended purpose.

- **Transparency and explainability.** There should be transparency and responsible disclosure so people can understand when they are being significantly impacted by AI and can find out when an AI system is engaging with them.

- **Contestability.** When an AI system significantly impacts a person, community, group or environment, there should be a timely process to allow people to challenge the use or outcomes of the AI system.

- **Accountability.** People responsible for the various phases of the AI system lifecycle should be identifiable and accountable for the outcomes of the AI systems, and human oversight of AI systems should be enabled.

If you're looking at the technology

For me, the last AI principle is the most important.

To use AI, someone has to make a decision. Other people will then implement the technology, and a third group will then use the new tools to produce an outcome, regardless of whether it's good or bad.

At every single point in the process the computers will have done what they were told to do by their human controllers. It is simply unreasonable then to argue that 'a computer did it', no matter how complex the algorithm or how obfuscated the processing that led to the result.

One more cautionary tale

There is perhaps no better example of what happens when ethical principles, good governance and moral obligation are ignored than Robodebt, the Australian Government's highly questionable and unlawful automated system to recover overpayments. It matched information from the Tax Office with that of Centrelink, which administers many government services for the unemployed, disabled and more.

In September 2019 the government had spent just over $600 million on the scheme and claimed to have recovered nearly $800 million. However, this was far from reality.

Instead, in four years from 2016 to 2020, nearly half a million automated letters were sent in error to the unsuspecting public stating that they owed the government money. This led to a class action and the government being told to pay in excess of $1 billion by way of compensation.

It's also alleged that more than 600 vulnerable people have died as a result of this scheme. In my opinion, those responsible for its creation and implementation should face some very harsh consequences, but as they're well-connected former government ministers, I doubt they will.

Should your platform deliver such egregious outcomes, you may not be quite so fortunate.

Top SaaS tip: It's man *and* machine, not man *or.*

TESTING

Failure is part and parcel of the software world, and rather annoyingly, there's every chance that a change made to your code today will break something you wrote months or even years ago. In fact, you should probably assume that everything your developers do has the potential to cause an issue, ranging from something incredibly minor like a spelling error to something horribly major like your platform being shut down for some time.

And it doesn't even need to be a change to your code that does it. Simple maintenance activities can have horrible consequences. A former colleague used to tell of the time he worked for a local business. It was his first job in IT and he was charged with doing the backup. Times were simpler back then and all he had to do was go to a command line and instruct the computer to copy the contents of one drive to another. For several weeks he duly copied A to B, until one day he inexplicably copied B to A. It was a simple error that replaced the day's work with yesterday's backup.

Ahh, the importance of putting proper processes and procedures in place so that silly things like that don't occur.

Mistakes in software are inevitable because we're talking about a machine with literally millions of parts being created and maintained by a cast of many humans, few if any of whom are in full receipt of the facts, and most of whom simply don't have the capacity to understand everything even if they were.

I'm not being critical of my counterparts there. Big systems take on a life of their own after a while and it takes a village to keep them upright.

Types of tests

There are a few different varieties of tests, and while – like the development process – you're unlikely to be involved in the minutiae, knowing a little about what the team gets up to will do you no harm.

Unit tests

These are typically small, low-level tests that make sure individual bits of your application are doing what they should. They typically operate close to the code and are quick to run and cheap to automate. You'll eventually end up with many, many thousands of these being created.

Functional tests

Functional tests focus on the user side of the application, making sure the product delivers the expected outcome. What happens during the processing isn't part of the test and will need to be covered by a series of unit tests. You'll end up with many thousands of functional tests as well.

Integration tests

Given the complexity of modern applications, it's important to ensure all the little pieces work together. This is where integration tests come in. They typically require more of the application to be running when they're executed, so they're relatively expensive to run in terms of computing resources. You'll end up with thousands of integration tests too.

End-to-end tests

These try to replicate human behaviour in an application and typically relate to a more complex series of interconnected events and activities like placing an order and receiving a subsequent confirmation email. These are expensive to run.

You'll have few end-to-end tests and they're typically focused on major functionality.

Acceptance tests

Acceptance tests exist at the end of the chain and focus on business needs and rules. They need the application to be up and running. They may also attempt to measure the application performance from an end user perspective. You'll have many acceptance tests.

Performance tests

Many development systems have tiny amounts of data and few concurrent users. Performance tests are needed to emulate more real-world environments with vast amounts of data and major loads on the system. Performance tests are inevitably expensive to run. You'll have many performance tests.

Smoke tests

Smoke tests are the software equivalent of giving something a quick once over. Their goal is simply to ensure that the major bits and bobs are doing what they should. They're a handy quick check of the basics, and if all's well you can commit to a little more in-depth testing with your many functional and unit tests.

How much testing is enough?

I hope it's obvious, but just in case, the point of testing is to stop defective software being released. However, the reality is that you will knowingly, willingly and sometimes enthusiastically release defective software. Unless you have the simplest platform ever, it's inevitable.

Your team will inadvertently create bugs, and with a little luck you'll find them before your customers do. Then you'll try to fix as many of them as you can. But at some point, the law of diminishing returns will kick in and you'll stop testing the iteration that you have and you'll release it.

When will that be?

Only your own real-world experience can tell you that.

Once it's out and about in the big wide world your customers will obligingly present you with a load more problems and you'll be amazed at the huge number of bugs you didn't find, and some of them will be stunningly simple to reproduce. The reason is developers have a tendency to make something the way they see it and occasionally fail to consider the other ways in which a user might interact with a system.

Practically speaking then, there's no right amount of testing. There's just enough. Enough that you think what you've got is ready to put in front of some paying punters.

Enough is enough then, as Barbra Streisand and Donna Summer told us.

GOING LIVE

Okay, so that's that then. All the thinking, planning, development, testing, more development, more testing, yet more development, and yet more testing has finally got you to a point where you've built something your target niche will find interesting and may even pay for.

All you need do now is push it out the door.

As ever though, there are a few other technology subjects to address. Once these are out of the way, we can take a good long look at going to market.

I'm really looking forward to that. It's my favourite bit.

It's all about people.

Still, back to the technology for a few more pages.

It won't take long. I promise.

Congratulations

You're now the proud parent of a software product.

I am too. When we went live for the first time, the overriding emotion was relief, and I mean relief in the *thank fuck that's over* kinda way. It's nothing like the joy of becoming a real parent.

Getting over the line is an exercise in tolerance, patience, compromise, commitment and so much more. There are thousands of things to do, and the moment you draw that line in the sand, you can start writing the list of the next million things that will follow. Your MVP only contains a fragment of the many dreams and ideas you have.

Ongoing deployment

When you're in the midst of developing a platform, there's usually only one version of it. Coding, testing and everything else happens in one development environment.

Then you go live, and you immediately add a layer of complication because both best practice and common practice say it's wise to separate your development world from the one that delivers revenue. The reason for this is simply that it's all too easy for a silly little mistake to completely trash the joint. So it's best to give your customers a safe haven in which to use your platform, and your developers can carry on without the risk of upsetting too many people.

And this then leaves you with the big question of what to do next.

> **Top SaaS tip: Beware! Common practice isn't always best practice.**

More or better?

You'll already have a long list of features that didn't make it into the MVP. These should all be written in the 'more' column. This will soon be steadily augmented by those voracious customers who'll insist that you make more and more product features for them.

Trust me when I tell you this. Some of what they'll ask for is just plain bonkers.

Serious professionals will ask you for things that defy comprehension and make you question your sanity. They'll say things like 'Can it just do … ', as if saying 'just' in the middle magically makes it less insane or simpler to deliver.

I've lost track of the number of times I've thought, 'No it can't! Bugger off,' or wanted to send the email that says, 'Can I ask you a question? Is there any chance you'll just piss off?'

I seem to recall saying the first of those a couple of times too.

Happily, there is a subset of requests which can be given to Leroy. Leroy is a fine gentleman who's so named because the work he gets represents a low return on investment, or LROI. All of his endeavours will be delivered as one as part of the much-heralded version 13 … whenever that will arrive.

Then there's the list of known issues which will also begin to buckle under the weight of the same customers demanding absolute perfection from you. These should all be listed in the 'better' column, and are somewhat harder to ignore, although not impossible.

So, which to do first? Make more or make better?

Welcome to the eternal software dilemma of how best to use your limited resources. This is a problem faced by every venture I've been involved in, from the largest of multi-billion-dollar enterprises with thousands of developers around the world, all the way down to the youngest and smallest of start-ups with one developer in her Aunt Ethel's spare room.

Finding the right balance is tricky, and it's complicated further by the fact that not all issues are equal. Sometimes a customer will find a showstopper issue, scream for the emergency services, and it'll be all hands on deck making the world right again.

Delivery models

Now that the internet is suitably high speed just about everywhere, delivery has become so much simpler than it was. Even if your software needs to be installed on a PC or device, automated update mechanisms make it a comparatively simple world.

The bad old days

Way back when, just a few short years ago, managing versions was complex. We'd build a major version, say version 5.0, that was good enough and we'd ship it on a DVD. We'd then immediately start working our way through known and emerging issues to build a fix pack. Emergency patches were published for showstoppers in the interim, and after several months an updated DVD containing all the fixes in a minor new version, 5.1, would be released.

New development was done in a separate stream ready for the next major version and all fixes would be merged into that. Then we'd release when good enough and set about fixing it, and so the cycle would continue.

The good new days

The modern world offers a somewhat different approach, although there are still many creating products for Windows and Mac who'll follow the well-worn paths of yesteryear.

Most SaaS platforms are delivered in the browser, and the notion of versions is largely outdated. Today continuous incremental change is the vogue and CI/CD (continuous integration, continuous delivery and continuous deployment) is the mainstream option. Instead of a cyclical approach, developers just pick up the next bit of scheduled work and get on with it. As soon as it's complete it gets tested and, assuming all is well, it's added to the product.

However, this doesn't mean it's immediately sent out the door, although it could be if you're brave or stupid enough to do so, and as all grown-ups should know, there's a rather thin line between the two. It's best to have an alpha or pre-release environment or similar where a tested version can be used by your own team or some tame customers in a controlled environment, prior to being generally available.

You might at this point be wondering how wrong it can go, and so as not to disappoint, here's one from the archives of a former colleague.

A cautionary tale from the archives

Harry, not his real name, worked for a TV company, one of those that has a set-top box. One day he and his team fixed some issues with the firmware and prepared to distribute it to the many live customer boxes via the usual update mechanisms.

However, this particular update also contained an update to the update mechanism and it was only after they'd sent it out that they discovered they'd inadvertently broken it. And this, as you can well imagine, presented a tiny bit of a problem.

After all, how do you update the update software on thousands of devices when you can't send an update using the update?

Harry, being the ever-resourceful man that he is, after a few moments of panic and contemplation of his career choices, wandered down to the cybersecurity team and asked if there were any new security bugs that had been found of late. As luck would have it, they'd recently found a flaw that would allow anyone with knowledge of it to send code to the boxes and execute it.

Harry breathed a sigh of relief and set about hacking his own hardware, and for once, one of my cautionary tales has a happy conclusion.

SUMMARY

The development process itself is long, complicated and rather dull for those not working their fingers to nubs hammering out code, and if you're on the receiving end, it's likely going to feel like it's taking an eternity. That said, it's seriously exciting whenever you get to see a new feature come to life.

And that's why you hire a professional development team. They'll manage all of this for you, delivering little presents along the way, leaving you to focus your efforts on generating some interest and building a narrative about your platform and the value it's going to deliver to your soon-to-be-ecstatic clients.

Well, that's the plan anyway.

So, without further ado, let's put all this technical nonsense behind us and push on to the best bit: going to market. This is just as subtle and nuanced as all that's gone before, but for many of you, some of it will at least be far more familiar territory.

Top SaaS tip: Getting to market is far easier than staying there.

CHAPTER 6

GOING TO MARKET

At last! The fun bit. We're finally going to look at the human side of the business. I know we got a mention or two on the way through, but we're front and centre now. This chapter is all about how you, your business and your product can get out there and start earning you a crust.

That means lots of enthusiasm and effusive commentary about selling, marketing, how your solution is worth so much to so many, and how you can fight them on the beaches and bluster, bluster, bluster. Before all of that though, I've distilled all of the failures and broken SaaS and software dreams into a simple-to-digest list of seven mistakes. As you read through them, you may begin to reconsider a few things you thought were on the money just a couple of pages ago.

SEVEN COMMON MISTAKES WHEN GOING TO MARKET

Having a technology focus

If you're looking at the technology, you're missing the point.

I know I've said that before, and I bet I say it again before the end, but seriously, if you haven't worked out that this is all about the many people you're going to interact with, you're going to be in for a torrid time. This is all about solving human problems and delivering value. Nothing more and nothing less.

Having an unclear target

Developers cost money, a lot of money. So does marketing. Every potential customer who buys a competing product costs you money.

So, take the time to be absolutely crystal clear about who your target market is. Make sure you know every facet of their world, be it good, bad or ugly. The tighter your niche, the more accurately you can allocate your precious resources.

The wider you spread your net, the more it'll cost to fill it.

Believing if you build it they will come

No, they won't.

You are not Kevin Costner and neither are you making a baseball diamond in the middle of nowhere for a bunch of dead people to come play an imaginary game.

Check out *Field of Dreams*. It gets an 86% audience rating on Rotten Tomatoes, was nominated for three Academy Awards, including Best Picture, and it was selected for the National Film Registry. It is, objectively speaking, a really good movie. But it's still not going to get you the customers you need. That's going to take an effective content marketing strategy and not making the other six mistakes either side of this one.

Under pricing

More on pricing shorty, so suffice to say for the moment that the race to the bottom is something to avoid. Build a high-quality product, price it reasonably and accordingly, and put it in front of the right people. The good ones will happily pay for the value you offer.

Having poor after care

Seriously, if you're going to go to all that effort to make something to solve someone's problem, why would you sell it to them and then not bother to look after them? This is all about playing the long game and keeping your customers – do everything you can to deliver a five-star service.

Having a reactive development strategy

Your customers want value, value, *value*.

Giving customers what they want is fine, provided it's what they need. The list of things a customer wants changes with the seasons and sometimes the weather. Their needs, however, remain largely the same. So, give them what they need. You'll have a far more focused development effort and be far quicker to market.

Having too few referrals

Word of mouth and a personal recommendation are winners every time, so do everything you can to encourage your customers, fans, well-wishers and more to heartily endorse your offering. And when they do, give them a reward! Saying thanks is one thing and a few dollars discount one month is okay, but why not give them a discount for as long as their referral is a paying customer? I know of one vendor who does this. Some of his customers have so many referrals, they now get the product for free.

Top SaaS tip: Always play the long game.

VALUE

Way back in chapter three, I invited you to come to grips with a couple of simple ideas: what's the problem and whose is it? Hopefully by now the old grey matter has been toiling away and you have a good idea of what the answers are.

Sorry to say though, I've been a little less than forthcoming. The *what* and *who* give us a clear target to aim at. They help us ignore the superfluous, allowing us to focus on the core features. But, as important as they are, they're only half the story.

The time has now come to tell you the second half.

Also in chapter three I told you that value was an interesting notion and there'd be more about it later. Well, the time has arrived, and not a moment too soon because value and the delivery of it to your people underpins absolutely everything from now on. It might even make you reassess what's going to make it into your MVP.

Remember the drill bit analogy? We buy the bit to create the hole to put up the shelf on which to show off some pictures. It's the sort of job that doesn't really cost that much, even including materials and labour. The value though will likely be far higher, but this isn't determined by the shelf or the person constructing it but rather the recipient of the benefits that the shelf conveys.

So, a husband might ask his wife, 'Hey honey, would you like me to put up a shelf in the lounge?'

With no additional context, the value of the shelf is limited to it being a place to put something. But what if the wife is already thinking about needing somewhere for the pictures of the extended family and close friends? Now the value of the shelf is much greater because it has an emotional value attached to it, and while that might be hard to quantify in terms of a dollar amount, it's undoubtedly going to be worth so much more.

Defining such value in the business world can be hard too and it's not always easy to turn a concept into an amount, but we can at least use a couple of basic measures, and when we do we see just how much value can be delivered.

Basic metrics

There are three very accessible and understandable markers of value that usually make business leaders pay attention when you drop them into conversation.

The first is the $100,000 or so it costs to employ an average person for a year in Australia. Anything that means you don't have to spend big on humans has got to be good for the bottom line.

The second follows on from this and is the 150% to 250% of remuneration it takes to replace one of your people if they leave.

The third is the money they *won't* be spending on related things like office space, repairs, maintenance and a whole lot more.

Given how, when combined, these can represent some serious coin, you might also begin to wonder why so much software is so cheap to buy when it delivers so much value and costs so much to make. It's a very good question, and something you should keep in mind as I go through the list of some of the many ways in which software and technology add value.

Lots and lots of value

While I wrote this list with reference to how your platform can benefit your customers, think how many apply to your business and the tools *you* use. And if you really want to think big, consider how that value you create may even extend to your customers' customers. These are listed in no particular order and their relevance to a given business will depend entirely on circumstances. Your product can provide:

- **A more efficient team.** A team that makes fewer mistakes and gets stuff done is good for the bottom line.

- **A lower headcount.** If you're using technology, you won't need as many people to achieve the same outcome, and that's $100,000 for each wage you save.

  Of course, you can't say that in a sales environment, so it's far better to highlight how the customer would have additional resources it can use for income generation or to address other inefficiencies.

- **Reduced running costs.** A lower wage bill and fewer people mean less expenditure and reduced administration and infrastructure costs elsewhere in the business.

- **Slicker processes and procedures.** I urge you to invest in quality, and you should encourage your customers to do the same.

- **Greater productivity.** It's a fundamental value proposition of any technology. Use the tool and the team will get more done in less time. Whose boss doesn't want that?

- **More accurate information.** When a business decision made in error can cost millions, having the right information available has massive value, especially if it's available in a timely manner.

- **Better morale and a happier team.** Your team just wants to get their job done. Why make it harder for them? Give them the best tools and they'll be much happier, and that can increase productivity by as much as 12% according to Warwick University.

- **Improved staff retention.** If they're happier, they're less likely to leave, and remember, the cost of replacing a staff member is at least 150% of their salary.
- **A higher-quality team.** Your good team members are the ones most likely to find work elsewhere, leaving you with the not-so-good ones.
- **Smoother communication.** Technology delivers many ways to communicate. Where would we be without Zoom or Teams?
- **Greater working flexibility.** I first wrote this list long before Covid, so this one is doing way more heavy lifting than it used to now that working remotely is far more commonplace.
- **A more desirable working environment.** A happier team means it's a better place to work for everyone.
- **A cheaper wage bill.** People will do the same job for a lower wage if the working conditions are better.
- **Lower recruitment costs.** A better working environment means people are more likely to want to join, so you'll save on recruitment costs. Having lower wages might make them a little cheaper too.
- **Reduced business interruption.** Invest in quality and the business will keep running far more smoothly. Business interruption can be horrifically expensive, with downtime costing as much as three-quarters of a million dollars an hour for large enterprises.
- **Improved service standards.** 'I'm sorry sir, the system is really slow today,' is a guaranteed way to annoy any customer.
- **Happier customers.** Good service standards will lead to happier customers and they're far less expensive to look after than unhappy ones.
- **More customers.** Happier customers means better word of mouth, and that is always going to help attract new ones.
- **Lower customer churn.** Treat them well and they're less likely to drift away to a competitor and more likely to keep spending their hard-earned cash with you.

- **Increased revenues.** With a good system they might just use the platform more and spend more each time too.
- **Larger customer lifetime value.** The longer they stay and the more they spend, the better. This is a critical measure when compared to acquisition costs.
- **Cheaper customer acquisition costs.** Can your platform help customers onboard themselves? If it can, you get to use your human resources elsewhere, and when you scale you have one less problem to solve.
- **Reduced marketing spend.** More word of mouth means a better chance of closing a deal and less need to spend big to attract attention.
- **Greater transparency.** Accuracy of data and easier dissemination of information help you look so much better in the marketplace. Nobody likes dealing with a secretive organisation.
- **Smarter resource management.** If your tech means a business can better utilise its assets, you're saving them a small fortune in unnecessary expenditure on tools and people, and as I'm sure you know by now, everything to do with humans is just plain expensive.
- **Improved cashflow.** Businesses thrive on predictability. The more you can help them control their cash, the happier everyone will be.
- **Better integration with suppliers and partners.** Supply and value chain efficiency is worth countless millions. We need only look at the chaos caused by Covid to see this. The easier it is for businesses to work together, the better the outcomes all round.
- **Simpler collaboration.** Sharing documents, communications and more is commonplace today thanks to cloud services. Two businesses sharing processes and resources is even more valuable. I know this from experience at WiseTech, whose platform simplifies the logistics world, with customs data being entered once and then shared by many parties.
- **Ability to scale more easily.** Cloud-based solutions can be delivered at scale almost at will. For the growing enterprise, that's one less very expensive problem to solve.

- **A better reputation.** Looking after your people, whether they're customers, the team, suppliers, partners and more, will give your business solid appeal in whichever market we're talking about.
- **Reduced risk.** Last on the list is the slightly more amorphous notion of risk. If you can find a way to ensure a business won't spend a fortune on mistakes, and they're usually made by humans, you've got a lot to offer. Put this idea in the context of physical workplace safety or cybersecurity and you're offering massive value.

> Top SaaS tip: You'll be far more successful making friends than you will making enemies.

That's my list, and I hope it's given you a solid insight into how your platform can deliver a mountain of value. I doubt it's exhaustive though. Ultimately, the more familiar you are with your niche and their problems, the more value you can identify. And the more of that you can do, the more you can charge for your offering.

And that brings me on nicely to a couple of subjects that I tend to rant about a little whenever I'm on a podcast.

PRICING

While value is still at the forefront of our minds, let's consider how much you're going to charge for your platform, and to start, I'll make a very broad accusation.

In my opinion, nearly all software is sold way too cheaply. This doesn't mean you should immediately double the price, but then neither does it preclude it. If your value proposition is suitably robust, you'll be amazed at what a customer will pay.

Paying for value

I know from firsthand experience of a vendor whose customers can pay for additional features to be added to the platform as a priority.

Some years ago, analysis of their work showed that the quoted number of hours to implement changes was woefully inadequate and customers were getting new features added at great cost to the vendor.

The obvious way to solve the problem would be to adjust the estimated hours so the fee adequately covered the cost of development. However, the CEO took a different approach and simply doubled the hourly rate. You may think this might alienate the customers, but in reality it's a very pragmatic solution. His argument was this: the business could spend time and energy trying to get estimates right and most likely still get them wrong. The alternative would be to back themselves and the inherent value in the work they were doing and get the customer to pay more for it. And, because the customer was the instigator of the change, they had a vested interest in the functionality and would already have assigned a value to it of some sort. This value would be all but guaranteed to be far in excess of the cost of implementation.

With one simple change the problem has been solved, and most notably, no customer has ever complained about the price.

How it used to be

Way back when, there was little software around because there were very few computers. You might think I'm referring to the dark ages or the early days of the industry, but as recently as the late 1990s there really weren't that many options available. Windows was still very much in its infancy and competition among vendors was relatively small. To put this in perspective, when I went out to sales gigs in my pre-sales capacity for LANSA we would encounter the same two competitors almost without fail. The lack of available choices had the same effect that scarcity usually does on pricing and customers were happy, or at least happy enough, to pay top dollar. However, times have changed since then and there have been two significant contributors to the changes in pricing.

Personal computing

By the late 1990s, Windows and Mac were in their prime and everyone was building software that ran on them. Tiny 3.5″ diskettes had been replaced by CDs and easy to install and use software was in vogue.

And with them came the mass market for software. Quite how many packages were available back then is unclear, but it's safe to say it probably ran into the thousands.

What had been an almost entirely B2B (business to business) sales model with low-volume high-value deals had been augmented by a new B2C (business to customer) model, and vendors were loving it. Gone were the complex delivery models with consultants, training and more, and in came the shrink-wrapped box with CDs and manuals, and users were left to their own devices.

And higher volumes meant lower prices.

Mobile, mobile, mobile

The arrival of the Apple iPhone in July of 2007 and the subsequent launch of the App Store, the Android phone and Google Play changed the landscape once more, and the mass market for mobile software began in earnest.

When the Apple App Store launched in 2008 there were just 500 apps. By late 2011, there were 1000 times as many, and they had been downloaded a staggering 18,000,000,000 times. And many of them were just a few dollars to buy, and almost overnight software went from being an expensive commodity to a disposable toy.

Worse still – well, for software vendors anyway – was that many businesses were creating free apps for their customers. Of course, this makes complete sense as an app improves customer service levels and reduces costs elsewhere, but it also affected the public perception of software.

Apps vs Software as a Service

This is a problem for SaaS vendors because the person in the street doesn't really distinguish between a complex multi-tenant SaaS platform and a $5 app. As far as they're concerned both are instantly accessible and all you have to do is sign up. More annoying is that handy little utilities delivered in an app can be perceived as being far more valuable than a whole platform because often a customer will only use or encounter a small percentage of what's available.

There's clearly a disconnect then between the value of a platform and public perception, and this is why it's so important for vendors to really dig deep to find their niche and value proposition. The better you can become at talking with the right people and articulating the massive value your product delivers, the more likely it is you can charge a fair price for it.

A posh to-do list

By way of example, I'll tell you about Nick. He has a platform aimed at small businesses that allows them to create task lists for the team. Once created, team members can mark each of the items as complete. The manager can see this in real time, and also has a dashboard with statistics so they can monitor performance. I don't want to oversimplify what the platform does, but that's the gist of it from a functional perspective.

This might sound like it's little more than a to-do list and something you ought to be able to buy for a few dollars per user per month at most, but Nick charges a far bigger fee – and gets it. His value proposition is that by implementing the many predefined lists or creating your own, you can ensure that revenue-generating activities aren't forgotten by the team. For example, he has one customer who has an A-board that's put outside a store every day. If the team forgets it, fewer customers come in and revenues significantly drop. As this can be in the hundreds of dollars on some days, the investment in Nick's platform is well worth it if it ensures the board is put out every day.

Setting your price

When it comes to determining the number you're going to attach to your offering, there are several options. Quite which is best for you will depend on your needs at the time and may be subject to change as your business and the market evolve around you.

Cost-based pricing

Using your costs to determine price seems like a reasonable place to start. You work out how much you've spent on salaries, hardware and so on and then you make a best guess as to what each unit you sell has cost to make. Then you add on a healthy margin of say 30% and enjoy your profits.

Ahh, if only it were that simple.

The downside is that there are thousands of things that can derail this plan, including not selling as many as you expected. It also wilfully ignores what the competition is punting their wares for, and that will affect your sales pipeline.

Competition-based pricing

If you're the new guys or you're in a fiercely competitive space, setting your price based on those around you is a good way to start. You can always adjust as you go along. You certainly don't want to be seen as too expensive without justification, or too cheap so that prospects might question the value you offer.

It's worthy of note here that blindly trusting your perceived competition's price as a guide risks opening yourself up to a world of pain. If they're using a growth pricing strategy, they may be cheaper than normal. Or they may simply have a big pile of cash on their hands and can afford to buy their way to comparative success. Most notably, they may have blindly followed others, just as I'm encouraging you not to do, and who's to say whether that'll be enough to keep them going. They may just be setting themselves up for failure, and it wouldn't do for you to simply follow suit.

Freemium pricing

I have a love-hate relationship with the ideas behind freemium products.

Freemium refers to providing a free version of your product, with the idea that they will upgrade to a paid version of your product later. Customers can simply sign up at zero cost and get on with it, and in the mass market this is undoubtedly a way for you to attract a few users. The art of course is to make sure people have just enough platform to keep them happy. Too little and they'll drift away. Too much and they'll never upgrade their service to the paid version with its additional features and superior customer experience.

However, if you give something to someone for free, they never value it anywhere near as highly as something they paid for, and broadly speaking it devalues your product. They're also far less likely to be in your niche or target demographic and thus they're far less likely to buy into your brand value, and as you should always be playing the long game that's a suboptimal approach to client acquisition.

Worse though is that the free version typically becomes more functional over time as more features are added to the paid version, and this makes it far less likely that a customer will move up. This leaves the vendor in a ridiculous, self-made mess of having to continually service a stack of hungry freeloaders who deliver little by way of value other than being only slightly more likely to become a paying client than a random person picked off the street.

Freemium has its place of course and for start-ups it's a means of gaining traction, but in my experience it needs to be used sparingly and for a limited period. After all, your business costs money to run and venture capital is getting much harder to find.

Perhaps my biggest bugbear with free software, even as a loss leader, is that it exacerbates the devaluation of software more broadly, putting pressure on other vendors to do the same, and SaaS is hard enough as it is.

An alternative approach, and one I advocate for strongly, is to use the opportunity to make an impact and to connect with your community. If you don't want to make a dollar for yourself from it, fair enough. But rather than giving it away, why not ask for a one-off donation to fund a charitable impact aligned with your purpose?

You may choose to demand this before providing access, but better would be to request it after a couple of weeks of free use. Perhaps best is to show a regular prompt for a small donation that goes away once the money is paid. This allows prospects to try your platform, but doesn't prevent them from using it. Regardless of which you choose, the aim is to get your customers to help fund your purpose in exchange for the free product they're using.

Growth pricing

Early-stage businesses use growth pricing as a means to gain market penetration. Essentially this is little more than undercutting the competition, and while valuable in the short term, over time it becomes an increasingly risky strategy that makes you look less than reliable or desirable. You might as well have shouty ads on TV and big flashing signs saying '50% off'.

> **Top SaaS tip: If you win the race to the bottom, you may well lose everything else.**

Tiered pricing

Tiered pricing has changed. Years ago it was a reflection of the size of the machine on which the platform was implemented. The bigger the machine the more you paid.

Today it typically refers to the package of features. You might offer freemium, bronze, silver and gold packages, where freemium has the least and gold is everything. An alternative is that each tier may apply to different size businesses, so freemium, small, medium and enterprise levels, and be measured by the number of users.

Usage, users and features pricing

This is one of my favourite models, although it's a bit harder to implement.

Usage pricing allows you to apply a small fee to everything a user does. This way, those who use your product a lot will pay for the pleasure and those who don't pay very little.

This is particularly attractive for B2B platforms because there's no massive outlay up front and small businesses won't have to pay the same as enterprise businesses. There are usually just a few relatively small implementation costs and then an increased bill as it's rolled out across the business and the number of transactions grows. More importantly, as your customers grow, thanks in part to your brilliant software, they'll use it more and pay you more.

Quite how you slice and dice your offering to determine what and where to charge is entirely up to you. You might have a flat price per user per month for everything, offering discounts as the numbers increase, or sign up all potential users and only charge the active ones.

Similarly, you may split by feature or specific activities, similar to the way in which Facebook charges for an ad to be placed.

While this is a solid model, it's important to ensure you're still delivering great value. If the price keeps going up but the value remains the same or declines, you're setting yourself up for failure.

Value-based pricing

Hopefully the first few pages of this chapter gave you a good idea of what I mean by value, and for me, it's an excellent way to charge, especially if you have a niche B2B offering.

Aligning your price with the value you create for the client means you get to ignore the competition, what it costs to build and deliver your solution, and any other day-to-day factors. You're simply making an assertion to the prospect that no matter how exorbitant the price may appear, they'll get their money back quickly and a mountain more value on top.

> **Top SaaS tip: There's no such thing as a free customer.**

Capital vs operational expense

However you decide to price your product, it's worth noting that offering a subscription greatly enhances your chance of selling to business users.

Big-ticket one-off software purchases will always need to be approved by the appropriate officers as they are regarded as capital expenditure. However, smaller monthly payments – such as a software subscription – can often be absorbed by operational budgets, which means that a department manager can make a decision and get on with it without needing to chat with the IT team.

From the IT manager's point of view this is a bit of a horror show as they lose control, and the Shadow IT monster is unleashed. This of course isn't your problem specifically, but such activities can lead to internal angst and problems downstream, so it's worth being aware of, just in case. Implementations that don't ultimately go well will always reflect on you, regardless of whether that's fair or not.

Is that the right price?

Many years ago, when I was negotiating to buy my house, the vendor and I were quibbling over a few dollars here or there. Okay, so it was about $20,000, but it was a small percentage of the overall sale price. He was determined to milk every last cent out of me, and I had no intention of going beyond my second offer, which was 10% on top of my original offer, and funnily enough, about 10% more than I wanted to pay.

It was also about 10% less than they'd originally wanted, which is why they were pushing hard.

As the negotiations reached their climax the agent said to me, 'The price must be right because you're both hurting a little', and this is a sentiment that's stuck with me. The right price is often the one where you almost feel like you're giving it away and your customers are trying to get that last discount out of you.

Your clients will never want to pay what you think your product is worth, and just like buying a house, if the price seems too low they'll become suspicious that it won't deliver the value they need. This is just the way of things – c'est la vie.

What's most important is that you listen to feedback in whatever form it comes. For example, you might put up the price on your website and start getting fewer enquiries. If that happens, all you know is that something isn't quite right. The question is, what isn't right? That is where the art of pricing lies. Is it really too expensive, or are you not explaining the value sufficiently?

So, remember, the price you demand applies to the value you're offering, and while that's ultimately the nuts and bolts that you deliver, it's not what your marketing copy talks about. People pay for the value they can see.

Start-up pricing

Start-ups are caught between a rock, a hard place and a range of rocky hard places. They can go cheap and aim for growth, find some paying punters and hope that slow and steady wins the race, or they can pick from a range of positions in between.

The right choice is going to be the one that suits your business, your budget, your market, your [insert other consideration here] and so on. Given the failure rate of early-stage SaaS businesses, revenue generation needs to be a serious consideration. If you're not making money, you're spending your own and quite possibly someone else's, and that is a situation that risks coming to a quick and permanent end.

FEATURES, FEATURES AND MORE FEATURES

Unless your product is so super niche that you're the only game in town, there's a very strong likelihood that you have a few competitors, and by a few, I mean loads. I recall making a presentation a few years ago and talking about customers having a handful of major competitors and a few also rans to make up the numbers.

Not any more.

I've just looked at Capterra.com, which apparently has been helping businesses choose better software since 1999. At the time of writing it lists just under 1500 CRM (customer relationship management) products; 820 email marketing solutions; 430 helpdesk platforms; nearly 1400 project management tools; and that's just scratching the surface.

It has over nine hundred categories to choose from.

So, it's reasonable to assume that you're going to face stiff competition, and this begs the question as to how you'll stand out from the crowd. Banging on in your marketing copy about the many features you have available should not be high on your list of priorities.

Selling cars

Car advertising can teach us a lot about marketing strategies in a competitive market. After all, cars in the same class are all pretty much the same. Let's consider my new one, which is a mid-sized SUV family car. I bought it to replace an eighteen-year-old small to medium sized SUV.

Both have four wheels, a steering wheel, seatbelts, headlights, seating for five, an entertainment system, navigation, a spare wheel and so on, and you won't be surprised to learn that all the competitors to my new one have these exact features too.

Mine however has some particularly nifty technology and a few gizmos and gadgets that aren't on other vehicles. That said, some of them have features that mine doesn't have, or they're larger, or more economical, or whatever particular difference you care to highlight.

And that's the point.

If we look solely at the features we can very quickly get confused. The lists are nearly always largely identical with a few different items and a few minor changes to specifications here or there, and that makes it very hard to make a meaningful comparison. Of course, I spent a long time trying to do just that, but when all's said and done, I bought mine for one reason, and one reason only. I could tell you it was the suede upholstery, top-notch technology, performance, cooling seats (I never knew I wanted those until I found out they exist), tinting on the windows and a host of other worthy features. But it wasn't any of them. It was simply that when I took it for a test drive, I loved how it made me feel.

So, yep, you've got it. I spent tens of thousands of dollars on a new car because it made me happy. That might sound a tiny bit unhinged, but it's pretty much how all buying decisions are made. We have an emotional reaction to something and then we rationalise our behaviour to support our decision.

Top SaaS tip: We pay with the mind, but we buy with the heart.

Same, same ... but different

It's interesting to think that SaaS prospects are spending their time making feature comparison lists as they try to choose which of the 1500 CRM platforms to try and then buy. I can't think of anything more offensive to my tech sensibilities, but some people really like that sort of thing.

Each to their own, I suppose.

What I find even more interesting is that some vendors do the work for you. They have feature lists that compare their platform against their perceived major competitors. I understand why they do this, but I wouldn't.

The practice seems to stem from a belief that having more features for the same price is better than having fewer, but this is a somewhat limited perspective because it fails to consider quality. Perhaps most important is that it sends completely the wrong message to the prospect. Rather than connecting them with an emotion and helping them feel good about their purchase, they are instead confronted with a completely impassive list of what are little more than commodities, and they're always bought on price. In effect, the vendor is saying you can only judge us based on this one dumb comparison and nothing else matters, and that effectively means they're all but selling on price and racing to the bottom.

Selling the 10%

Not all prospects are buying a new solution though. Some will be solving a problem they've solved before, so they're often doing little more than choosing a replacement for an existing package.

This scenario dilutes your value proposition dramatically. The problem you now face is that not only do you have to convince them to pick you over the rest, you also have to convince them your offering is better value than their incumbent solution which already delivers 90% of their needs, and perhaps even 100%. It may be that they're simply transitioning from an older now defunct solution to a modern one.

In such scenarios, you're only selling the extra 10%, which often means prospects are more sensitive to price. That's all the more reason to keep talking about value and how great their life will be once they've made the right decision to go with you. This is easier said than done in a sales meeting though, especially when confronted with someone who's only concerned with the price. Still, if there's one thing experience has taught me about prospects who buy on price, it's that they're rarely if ever good customers and really not worth the effort of trying to close the deal.

Feature preachers

While I'm on the subject of features and selling, I must tell you about an affliction that's shared by many vendors small, large, young or old. It's one that costs them time, money, opportunity and, most of all, sales.

It's an obsession with creating extra bells and whistles for no good reason.

One of the more common scenarios that plays out inside the walls of SaaS businesses is when the salespeople complain to product managers, the development team and anyone else who'll listen to their woe-is-me sob story that they could sell so much more if only they had this one extra feature. They tell tales of how their prospects and customers tell them that the product is seriously lacking, that the opposition has this bell or that whistle, and without it you just can't be taken seriously in the market.

Now you might at first think that such arguments and protestations are entirely reasonable, but if your product serves a high-value, low-volume vertical market or you're selling it as part of a wider service offering, I'm inclined to suggest you pay little more than lip service to such demands. And that's my polite way of saying I call bullshit.

You shouldn't dismiss them out of hand of course, and when their sales targets are being hit, missing features will barely rate a mention. But experience tells me they're little more than excuses. They're a reason a salesperson will use to justify why a few deals have fallen through the cracks, and to take your focus away from the fact that many of their other prospects also haven't closed.

This will also be used as an excuse by low-grade prospects as to why they're not going to buy and this is usually a sign that they're a bit of a tyre kicker. After all, do you really think that all the other great value you offer is outweighed by one missing bit of functionality?

If that alone isn't enough to keep you on the straight and narrow of eschewing extra shiny things in favour of a focus on need and delivering value, consider this. You can only use your resources once, and that means you're going to have work out where best to spend your hard-earned cash. This means you get to choose between splashing out on a bunch of development resources for a bit of techno-whimsy or paying for a heap of sales and marketing activity. If the lion's share is being allocated to fulfilling the whims of a loud minority for the sake of an extra sale or two, there's every chance you're not going to get the best bang for your buck.

Much better then to focus your energies on making sure your developers are pointing at the right problem and that your marketing engine is doing all it can to fill your funnel with high-quality prospects. Then your sales team can keep themselves well out of the weeds and instead talk about the problems you solve and the fantastic business outcomes and value your product already delivers.

That is, after all, precisely what you pay them to do.

So, give scant regard to the feature preachers and their demands for more bells and whistles, because you've got far better things to do than listen to those who bang on about the one thing you got wrong rather than the many you're getting right.

ARTIFICIAL INTELLIGENCE ... AGAIN

In the previous chapter I gave you a heads up about the many concerns and difficulties you'll face if you try to develop AI functionality. This time around, I'm going to take your prospective customers into consideration.

There are quite a few AI services you can use for machine learning and natural language processing such as Google's Vertex and OpenAI, and I have no doubt that you'll be more than ethically virtuous in all that you do should you decide to use them.

The question you have to ask yourself is whether advertising that you use AI is a good thing.

My suggestion is that it is not.

As previously discussed, AI is still very much in its infancy and has a poor track record that quite rightly makes many scared of what it might lead to. Now, to be abundantly clear, an army of Arnold Schwarzenegger lookalikes armed to the teeth with phased plasma rifles in the 40-watt range isn't about to burst through the door, nevertheless it's a subject that causes concern.

Perhaps most important is that your customers most likely don't care whether you use AI within your systems any more than you care about the finer details of how your car engine conserves fuel when stationary. They, like you, are simply happy that the system works and produces a beneficial outcome.

Trust is also a major concern for many. Those who've seen *Little Britain* may recall the 'computer says no' sketches, where unsuspecting customers are confused and confounded by systems that defy common sense at every turn. Or there's my favourite example from the magnificently funny *Rise and Fall of Reginald Perrin*, where the results for an exotic ice-cream flavour survey are returned in just two minutes by the computer. The three chosen flavours are 'book ends, pumice stone and West Germany'.

These may be comedy gold, but they're also indicative of the distrust many have with automated systems, and it's why I recommend that you don't use the .AI domain name for your product, unless of course you happen to be developing a specific algorithm, in which case, go for your life.

If you must crow about the tools and techniques you use, say something generic about 'using the latest and greatest technologies'. That way you're not boxing yourself in.

SELL SOFTWARE NOT PROMISEWARE

One of the common problems I see in vendors that have made it to market is they can lose faith in their product when sales volumes decline. They wouldn't necessarily call it that, but it's what it looks like to me as an outsider. They have a platform that delivers value but, for whatever reason, they're not selling as much as they used to or want to, so they start looking for scapegoats and ways to arrest the decline.

They consider cutting the price or developing new modules to make the platform more robust, the latter of which is fine if it's something that's properly aligned to their core value propositions. The only problem is that such things take time to deliver, sometimes many months and years, and going to market with 'promiseware' is a risky strategy for the customer and for you. If for whatever reason the promises fail to materialise in a reasonable timeframe, and there are plenty of opportunities for failure like losing core developers or it just being way more complex and harder than you imagined, your customer is going to be less than pleased. Apart from the significant reputational damage there's likely to be a financial penalty too.

One more cautionary tale

It was the early days of the internet back in the late 1990s and just about every tool vendor was jumping on the bandwagon, LANSA included. It had a new feature that turned existing applications into something that could run in a browser with little more than a change of one value.

This was heady stuff back in the day, I can tell you.

I remember demonstrating the product to a prospect and they seemed very pleased. However, a few days later Paul the sales guy came back from a meeting incandescent with rage. The prospect had been offered a ludicrously cheap price to go with a competitor whose web solution hadn't yet made it to market and in fact wouldn't be ready for six months or so.

It got to market eventually – but it took several years. Unsurprisingly, the customer couldn't wait and got their money back. They also turned up again at LANSA, although this time with different people.

They only wasted two years or so.

FIVE-STAR SERVICE

Building software that can solve a customer problem is a solid start, but if you're not going to back it up, you're going to do both your client and you a thorough injustice.

As ever, relatively simplistic mass-market products can get away with the bare minimum, but everyone else has an obligation to deliver a good level of service, and it should start long before a prospect becomes a customer. In fact, good service should be a major part of everything you do, from first contact right through to delivery and beyond.

It starts with a digital hello

If you're looking at the technology, you're missing the point.

See. Told you I was going to say it again. It won't be the last time either.

So, forget for a moment that you're selling a tech solution and instead pretend you invested in a boutique on your local high street. How might the various types of customer compare? Most people on the street will walk past your store paying it no attention whatsoever. They're going somewhere else and they're looking for something different. There are billions of people just like them searching the internet daily and they'll never land on your website.

Some might stop and have a look in the window, and doubtless you'll have made some effort to make it look attractive and to highlight something you're keen to sell. They pay just enough attention to put you in a pigeonhole and then they carry on about their business. These are the people who see your website listed somewhere, or perhaps encounter some content or advertising.

Some might come inside and have a look around at your wares. These too will be well laid out, in an aesthetically pleasing and understandable order. They may pick things up, touch them, smell them, and read the tickets and labels. They'd probably enjoy a quick hello from the team, and they may enquire about your products or ask you general questions about a particular problem they're trying to solve. These are equivalent to the people looking through your website.

Those who think you have the right solution for them will make a value judgement and some will happily pay for their goods and become a customer.

I use this analogy for the simple reason that it's familiar to all of us, and we all know the kind of service we'd like to receive.

Your digital boutique should be no different. The shopfront should be just as attractive, and when a prospect comes in they should be able to browse easily and find all the information they need.

And just like a bricks-and-mortar store, a 'hello, how can we help?' will go a long way.

Implementation models

Most SaaS platforms are what's referred to as 'multi-tenant'. Such systems are designed to support multiple customers and multiple users, with each often distinguished by email address or another identifying attribute. Everyone signs in and they all receive much the same experience. It may be that the product can be configured for each customer, but the underlying structure remains unchanged.

Multi-tenant platforms usually mean that everyone is effectively sharing the same set of infrastructure. The obvious downside here is that if there's a problem, say with a cloud vendor like Amazon which hosts about a third of the internet, we're all in big trouble until they get themselves sorted.

I know that sounds scary, and you may well wonder why on earth you'd willingly put yourself in that position, but it's perfectly normal these days and you can pay it no mind. Those who deliver internet infrastructure are very good at what they do. They're little different to other utility providers like water and electricity.

Shared infrastructure will do just nicely for most clients, but some larger businesses may want the option to run your software on their own kit. This is referred to as an on-premise solution. The software remains the same, it's just installed on a different set of computers. There are hybrid alternatives too if you want to get really complicated.

The good news is that I'm telling you this just in case it comes up in conversation – you can probably safely assume your tech team is all over such things. It might be worth checking though, just in case. It's also worth noting that if you're selling to the kinds of business that wants to run on-premise, they'll be big enough that money will likely be little or no object.

Top SaaS tip: The bigger the prospect, the more they understand value.

Training

The more specific your solution, the more important it is for you to have a robust set of training programs and a wide variety of delivery models.

Onsite, in-person, instructor-led programs are still common for more complex and in-depth requirements. This is how nearly all courses were run when I was a trainer way back when, and I still believe they give the students the best chance of success. Being able to discuss scenarios with another human, especially an expert, provides far more nuanced answers and insights.

It is possible to run similar programs remotely, but it leads to a different dynamic. Zoom and other video platforms enable screen sharing and 'face-to-face' interaction, but it's just not as good as the real thing, and it can lead to 'Zoom fatigue', which is an increasing problem for remote and hybrid workers.

The mainstream today is student-led online courses. These are delivered using a combination of written words with supporting images, instructor videos, screen captures with voiceover and of course exercises to help embed the learning. We all learn using a variety of stimuli and inputs, so the more options you make available, the better it will be for all.

Don't underestimate the importance of training your clients. The more familiar they are with your offering, the happier they'll be, the less they'll call you for support and the more likely it is they'll tell others about you.

Word of mouth is still the choice of champions.

As with so many of the subjects that this book touches on, I'm just scratching the surface. The creation of training programs is a specialist skill. There are tools and learning management system (LMS) SaaS platforms to help you do it yourself, but it's a lot of hard work and you're almost certainly going to need some help.

I told you at the start this was an expensive game.

My last word on training, at least for the moment, is to remind you of the oft-repeated tale of the supervisor concerned about the cost of training and that the team might leave for a better job. He mentions it to the boss who simply replies, 'I'd rather train them and have some leave than have a load of untrained people who won't.'

Help

It's impractical to create training courses for every single facet of your product. So no matter how in depth they are, they're only ever the beginning of the education process. Apart from that, no one really wants to go through structured learning just to understand the meaning of a particular box on the screen. This is where help text comes in.

Your help text will be the first port of call for the majority of your customers. Most people prefer to simply look something up as they need it rather than submitting a support request or talking to a representative. It should provide specific and detailed assistance on every single bit of your product (I once had the pleasure of writing over 4000 individual bits of help), as well as associated information to help the user understand the whys and wherefores of everything they see.

Like training material, writing help is a bit of an artform and it can and should be delivered using many different media. Perhaps most important is that it's contextual. Being able to press F1 or click help on a control or for a particular screen artefact means the user sees what they need to see straightaway without having to perform a search.

Why is that so important?

Because many customers won't know what to search for, and that being the case, the chance of them finding helpful information is greatly reduced. This is one of the reasons I advocate for you to create a glossary. If you get into good habits, you can make one as you go. It doesn't need to be complex: just an explanation of the word and a couple of common synonyms if you have them.

Top SaaS tip: Relying on assumed knowledge makes us all look dumb.

Support

If training hasn't supplied the requisite knowledge and your reams of help text haven't either, your customers will soon be knocking on your door asking for assistance. The questions they'll ask, suggestions they'll make and rants they'll go on will exceed your wildest dreams and nightmares. I once spent forty-five minutes on the phone dealing with a customer complaining that we'd broken his end-of-month processing. Apparently, it had worked perfectly last month but not this one. In the end, the difference turned out to be a change he'd made two weeks previously, but I'd had to trawl through his code to find it.

Support comes in a variety of forms, including phone, email and live chat. Having a public user forum for discussion can add excellent value too, especially if your team contributes to the conversation. Remember also that every problem customer A has is a potential problem for customer B. If you can find a way to expose the details for wider consumption, you're taking a little bit of weight off your own shoulders.

Whatever you do, don't scrimp on your support team. Beyond your website and social media content, they are the human face of your business. When your customers are stuck and can't move forward, they'll come to you in the hope you can free them. When they find something that doesn't work, you can help them find a workaround. Your support is where you can show how much you love your people, no matter how bonkers some of them are.

Experience tells me that much of your support effort will be spent on the loud people at either end of the capability spectrum. The mainstream of your users, or the silent majority as I typically refer to them, will likely remain just that, finding and consuming the many alternative ways in which you share your wisdom.

Evangelists

For more complex and valuable platforms, the mantra must be that implementation is everything. It doesn't matter how good your tool is, how in depth the training, how immediate your support or how accurate your help, if your users aren't proficient and engaged there's going to be problems.

The best way to help with this is to appoint evangelists. These can be your people or they can come from the client, but either way, they'll be your eyes and ears and boots on the ground. They're a trusted resource and single point of contact you can embed at a client, and they are invaluable to both you and the customer. Evangelists are your local experts. Their job is to know everything there is to know about your platform and how best to leverage its value. In effect, they are the bridge between you and the customer, the human face of an otherwise remote and sometimes faceless digital experience.

If they're your people, they may well be viewed as an expensive addition to the cost of your platform, and something the customer can sometimes be a little too keen to avoid paying for. They often don't want to cough up for training either but avoiding both is a false economy. Convincing them of this may be hard though, but that's why I bang on so much about value, and why you should too. The value proposition for both training and evangelists is the same and should be regarded as a win–win scenario by both parties.

FINDING CUSTOMERS

Now that you're ready to deliver exceptional service and to do justice to both your customers and the exemplary product you offer, it's probably time we had a quick peek at the world of marketing and customer acquisition.

First of all, I'll appropriately cover my posterior and tell you to get out there and find some proper marketing help. Like so many of the adjunct activities of a SaaS business, this is one for a professional who understands the detail far better than I do. My job as ever is to raise your awareness and to ensure you're not wandering into a conversation with no preparation or ammunition.

So, with that in mind, my top ten activities will follow along shortly.

Before that though, a quick aside about top tens and their ilk. You can, and should, do your own research, and when you do you'll find there are many other views and opinions which will verify everything I write and probably refute a fair bit too. Things I consider important are just that. They're based on my experience, research, opinion and so on, and they may not rate a mention on others' lists.

In a similar vein, a *Harvard Business Review* meta-analysis of opinion on technology and the potential for job creation or destruction found that opinion was divided roughly down the middle and the consensus was that no one really knows what's going to happen.

Marketing is no different. As either merchant John Wanamaker in the US or possibly industrialist Lord Leverhulme in the UK is alleged to have said, 'Half the money I spend on advertising is wasted; the trouble is I don't know which half.'

Ten SaaS marketing tips

- **Know your buyer.** Knowing whose problem you're solving is essential for building software. Knowing who has the power and capacity to buy is essential for selling. Make sure you target the right audience.

- **You're unique, but … .** Unique selling points are great. They help you differentiate your product from the competition. But don't labour the point. What you're offering is a lifestyle choice, something that will change the lives of the buyer, and that's so much more valuable than a single point of difference.

- **Bang the drum.** It is loud out there in the market. Businesses of all shapes and sizes are screaming their version of 'Strawberries! Pound a punnet!', and spending big in the process. But, your niche is out there just waiting to hear from you, so start banging the drum and keep banging. They will hear.

- **Form a consistent narrative.** You know so much, and you have so much to offer. Sadly though, the ears that hear don't have the capacity to consume it all. So, pick your topics and focus on the essence of your offering.

  Remember, people don't buy drill bits.

- **Measure, measure, measure.** Whatever you do, measure it. Record what you do, when you did it and what the reaction was. Google, Facebook and all major platforms have data available for you to consume and consider.

  While you're about it, measure what your software does too. Some guidance on this will come along in the next chapter.

- **Use multiple channels.** Email, Facebook, Twitter, LinkedIn, Google, Bing, television, cold calling, shouting on the street corner or whatever. The more places you're seen by your buyer, the better.

- **Use different media.** Google's zero moment of truth (ZMOT) suggests that, on average, a prospect will spend seven hours researching and consuming content and need eleven different touchpoints in four different locations to make a decision. Seven hours is a lot just for text, so make videos, audio material and whatever else you can think of. Variety is after all the spice of life.

- **Sell your platform not your content.** If you have great content to share, share it. Don't hide it behind a pay wall. You'll spend your time trying to sell access to your wisdom rather than the brilliant software your team has made.

- **Reviews and testimonials.** Where do you think five-star reviews on Google and client testimonials come from? Do you think people just give them? Some might if you're lucky, but if you want such things, it's best to ask.

  And here's a tip within a tip. Make it easy for them. If you want someone to say your software has changed their life, ask them to send you a testimonial saying exactly that. You'll be amazed how often they will.

- **Shout about results.** Don't assume knowledge. If you're producing outstanding results and delivering massive value, and you can prove it, tell everyone.

  I know a vendor who gets an average 90%+ happiness rating for the events as part of his service. Being able to display that all over your marketing material is gold.

Two-sided markets

Reaching out to your niche is hard enough, but what if you have a solution that aims to serve two vastly different groups of people?

Do you have to favour one over the other?

From a sales and marketing perspective, the answer is a resounding yes. But which one?

Happily, there's a simple way to work this out.

The profusion of food delivery services connecting food vendors and consumers will serve as an excellent example. There are plenty of restaurants and takeaways, so attracting vendors is a relatively simple activity. The delivery service offers to sell their food for them for a percentage of the price. The only cost to them is a little effort setting up a menu, and perhaps a few pictures.

The challenge then is to convince the masses they want to have food delivered. Happily, they've been doing this for years anyway, so it's really an exercise in letting people know that all their favourite food delivery options are available in one place rather than having to thumb through multiple trifold takeaway menus, many of which are probably out of date anyway.

Now consider the value proposition for the two sides.

The food vendor saves time and energy and gets their product to market, but it's a somewhat transactional activity and the value is mostly financial.

The purchaser however is hungry. They don't want to go out, and they're hungry, or they can't, and they're hungry, and they're not about to cook for themselves, and yep, they're still hungry. If they don't get something soon, they'll be tucking into the cat food they're that bloody hungry.

For them, this isn't just a transaction. It's an emotive, almost life-and-death situation.

Now take a moment to remember that first bite of your favourite takeaway, the one you always get when you want to heal your soul. The one that's your go-to choice after a long day at work, or the one you look forward to when it's time for a little self-indulgence. (For me it's a chicken tikka masala with pilau rice and keema naan from my local Indian restaurant. Perfect with a couple of cold beers.)

Think about your hunger subsiding, the warmth spreading through you as you enjoy every mouthful, and the delightful flop on to the couch once you've gorged yourself. Consider that for just a few extra dollars you can have all of that brought to you with just a few clicks.

Now that's what I call value!

And therein lies the wisdom. This is, as I keep saying, little to do with the technology and all about humans. So, when it comes to two-sided markets, the lion's share of your resources should favour whoever gets the most value.

Selling

There's an almost endless supply of material available that will tell you how to sell your wares. It tells you how to sell business to business, how to sell ecommerce, how to sell if you're a start-up, how to sell if you're not, how to sell like a pro, and many more variations on the theme. And there are frameworks galore too, including the Bowtie model, which seems to be very popular at the time of writing.

Will it endure?

Who's to say?

But if there's one thing we can all be sure of, it's that something new will come along and it will doubtless be superior to all that's gone before. After all, it's hard to believe that today, right now, as I rattle away at the keyboard, we as a species have reached peak sales skills and there's nothing left to learn and no new approaches to try.

So, with our inevitable future in mind, I'm going to quickly skirt around the area of sales and selling and suggest that you engage specialist skills, support and education to help you manage your sales. I've been in this industry for a long time, and while I've been exposed to a great deal of selling in one form or another, I have but a passing knowledge and I'm most definitely neither a marketer nor a sales guy, just as those who promote their selling and marketing skills are rarely if ever software people.

Five tips for selling

Still, as this is a book for the layperson, and you may well be just as good at selling as I am, I thought I'd share five of the lessons I've learned over the years. I was taught all of these long before I ever realised that if you're looking at the technology you're missing the point. Now that I have, they seem strangely apt.

Don't show up and throw up

Nobody likes *that* sales guy. You know the one. He turns up with a tailored PowerPoint presentation with your logo and corporate colours, and then proceeds to tell you all about the features of the product and how it's the best on the market and blaargh!

As I'm sure I've repeated a few times now, you're not selling features. You're selling the massive value you deliver and a solution to someone's problem.

People buy people

This was my first proper lesson from a sales professional, back when the year began with a one. It was true then and it's true today.

First and foremost, we're all human, and whether you're selling indirectly via a website or in person, you're still dealing with other people. So you can forget all the sales nonsense and instead just be yourself. I've found over the years that being sincere, honest, passionate, authentic and knowing what you're on about is an excellent way of doing business.

Two ears and one mouth

This was my second proper lesson.

You have two ears and one mouth and when selling you should use them in that proportion. Translated this means you should listen twice as much as you talk, and of course this makes perfect sense. Your job is to find out all about the prospect, their problems and what they need and want. Once you know that you can explain how your solution resolves them all.

Don't sell to the wrong prospect

I know you want the money but selling a solution to someone who'll neither make good use of it nor appreciate its true value rarely ends well for either party. You'll waste your time and effort working on a deal that has a low lifetime value when you could be finding a far more lucrative one, and there's every chance the customer will never have anything good to say about you either. All in all, it's a false economy.

Ask for the business

All that effort qualifying and getting to know your prospect. All that time taken to listen and to explain how your solution will deliver exceptional outcomes. And then you shake their hand and go home?

Like most fish, SaaS prospects are unlikely to just jump into your net, so when you've answered all their questions, be sure to ask them one in return. Ask them if you can have their business.

You'll be amazed at the difference a simple question can make.

Top SaaS tip: Sell to *your* people, not all people.

Growth hacking

This is a term you'll likely encounter while you're rummaging around in the SaaS world. It's typically used to describe the low-cost activities of start-ups as they try their very best to build and maintain a customer base.

Quite what constitutes growth hacking is somewhat unclear, and the tips from the previous section will almost certainly be part of it. To my mind though, it's really a mindset more than anything. If you're focused on growing your business, you'll use just about every technique under the sun to achieve it, whether that's a social media push, advertising, asking your mum to tell her friends and more.

Giving away something for free seems to be an immensely popular and effective mechanism, though you should note I said *something*, not everything.

Dropbox did this by giving away free storage to anyone who signed up a friend. LinkedIn did it by allowing people to create a profile that meant they had a decent chance of showing up on the front page of a Google search, as I do when you search for Stewart Marshall. And Hotmail did it by adding 'PS I love you. Get your free E-mail at Hotmail' as a footer on the emails sent from its platform.

But perhaps my favourite is PayPal – and it was just plain smart. It gave $10 to every new customer. That sounds like a recipe for disaster and going out of business until you consider that their stats suggested that every customer they acquired was worth around $20.

Every $10 they spent would double their money.

Top SaaS tip: Blow your own trumpet because no one else will.

SUMMARY

Going to market, whether that's an MVP released to early adopters or your first day on the market proper, is arguably the hardest part of being a SaaS creator. It's certainly the most emotionally charged in my experience. Years of digital blood, toil, tears and sweat are rolled out as a digital platform and all you can do is hope it's all been worth the effort.

It is, as Winston Churchill said, the end of the beginning, and just as he ordered that church bells across the nation should ring out in celebration of the victory at El-Alamein, so you owe it to yourself and your team to shout your successes from the rooftops.

The problems you're solving are human and only your people will ever be able to appreciate the difference you can make to their existence. But they won't do that if they don't know about you, and in the crowded world of modern technology, hoping they'll find you by accident, work out how you can help and then spend big as well is a strategy that probably won't end well.

So get out there and make the most of this moment, angst and all. Tomorrow is coming whether you like it or not, and you're a parent now with a child to look after.

Top SaaS tip: Features for show, sales for dough.

CHAPTER 7

OWNERSHIP

Congratulations!

You've conceived, designed, built and released your SaaS platform to the public.

Now the rest of your life begins, and you have a baby to keep alive, a growing family to feed, prospects to find, customers to appease, partners to schmooze and of course your team has millions of lines of code to write.

You've become a technology parent and the buck, which until now had been relatively small, has started to get much bigger. And it still stops with you. Your customers now rely on you, and if you fail, they may too.

It's unlikely, but, you know.

No pressure!

The worst thing about your new situation is there are no manuals that will tell you what to do. People like me will offer our perspective in books and articles. We'll try to make helpful suggestions, point out where we went wrong and hope you'll absorb our lessons, but just like being the parent of a real child, there'll be a little too much making it up as you go along for comfort.

I remember bringing my daughter home for the first time. We carried her into our apartment in the baby capsule and then realised we had no idea what to do with her, or when the parenting would start, so we put her on the coffee table while we had a cuppa and considered our options.

Still, you have one distinct advantage. You've been actively involved in growing your child, so you have a long list of things to be getting on with that you already know quite a lot about.

A FACE ONLY A PARENT COULD LOVE

There are few parents who'd describe their child as ugly. They're always beautiful, and even if they're perhaps not the most aesthetically pleasing of children, they always have other attributes that shine through.

This appears to be human nature and we all do it.

Our emotional attachment transcends such superficial judgements because love is blind. Evolution it seems has quite cleverly discovered that our caring for our young gives them a far greater chance of survival.

And then there are OPKs – other people's kids.

You know the ones. The unruly, scruffy little urchins roaming the street, playing in the gutter, generally causing a disturbance and doing their level best to look like they belong in *The Beano*. I'm sure I grew up with a few of them, and I probably was one at some point; well, at least as far as someone else's mum was concerned.

That's the thing about perspectives. We each have our own, and our objectivity returns when we have no skin in the game.

So now let's think about software for a moment – specifically yours.

You will likely be entirely enamoured by your digital progeny and your love will be just as blinding as it is for your human child, should you have any. You'll probably ignore its many obvious flaws and fail to truly understand its inadequacies. You may even think everyone else should forgive its shortcomings, appreciating its inner beauty instead.

Yeah … that ain't gonna happen.

Your baby is going to judged and it's likely to be brutal, and they won't spare you necessarily by talking behind your back. Shitty reviews from dissatisfied customers and honest feedback during demonstrations are really going to hurt.

Never mind. It will be water off a duck's back … eventually.

Of course, they'll probably be telling the truth, so hard as it may be, you're going to have to learn to manage it.

WHAT'S NEXT?

A few home truths are sadly just the tip of the iceberg. Your MVP or version 1.0 of your platform represents just a fragment of all that's to come, and you're going to have a lot on your plate in the coming years.

And this means it's time for me to introduce you to …

The most important skill ever!

We all have room for a little personal improvement, and if there's one skill you should practise whenever you get the chance, it's saying *no*.

This is one of those times when you should trust my experience, wisdom and been-there-and-done-that-ness absolutely and without question.

I strongly recommend you indoctrinate your senior leadership too.

Being able to deny an insistent customer is the singularly most valuable and satisfying skill ever.

As I pointed out previously, customers have needs and wants. The former are understandable and sensible and will align with the fundamental vision and value propositions on which your platform is based.

The latter will range from sensible to mildly mental and may include the liberal use of 'just'.

They also have expectations, and they'll range from reasonable to bat-shit crazy, are rarely based on anything other than wild opinion and nearly always include the word 'should'.

So, the general rule of thumb is to focus on delivering solutions to cover needs first, and then look after the wants. You might throw in the odd sweetener now and then though.

> Top SaaS tip: We all deserve a treat from time to time.

Beware though. If you spend time addressing ridiculous demands just to get a sale or to calm the beast, you risk creating a millstone that you'll have to drag around forever. The more you acquiesce, the bigger and heavier, and thus more expensive and problematic, it will become.

So how does one avoid this situation?

Ask your mum, especially if she's one of those no-nonsense sorts, because it's one of the first things a parent with a small child learns. You learn to set boundaries. You learn to manage expectations. You learn to remain in control.

If you don't, your kids might just become spoilt brats, always getting their own way and likely having a tantrum when they don't.

And that's no fun for anyone.

So, do yourself a favour and learn to say a very firm *no!*

Bugs

Just so we're all on the same page, I'll quickly define what a bug is. For the moment, I'll use the definition as supplied by Wikipedia: 'A software bug is an error, flaw or fault in the design, development, or operation of computer software that causes it to produce an incorrect or unexpected result.'

Excellent. That seems nice and straightforward. Nothing complicated there.

Or is it?

Sorry to say, but the world of the software bug is not as clear cut as one might like it to be, and there's some grey area that's well worth learning about because it might just dig you out of a hole one day.

Top SaaS tip: If you find yourself in a hole, always dig up.

If software crashes, it's a bug. If it doesn't add up some numbers correctly, save your data when you tell it to or it lets you enter a date of 31st of February, it's a bug.

It's the bit in the definition about referring to a flaw in the design that I take issue with, because so many things that we create are used by other humans and we tend to be somewhat subjective sometimes.

Working as designed

To demonstrate this, I'll use an example from my past.

LANSA has its own language for coding and it's syntactically correct to write the following:

#A #B := #A + 1

For anyone with coding experience, this will be vaguely familiar syntax. It's an instruction to change variables A and B to the value of A with one added to it. Thus, if A is 5, the result would be that both A and B change to 6.

Easy right?

You'd think so, but not so fast, because that's not the case. For reasons that are lost in the mists of LANSA history and largely irrelevant anyway, what happens is that A is changed to A + 1, so 6, and then B is also changed to A + 1. The problem is that A has already been incremented, so B becomes 7.

This is far from world ending, but it was known to cause a problem or two for the unsuspecting, who'd immediately write an email reporting the bug, only to receive a reply telling them that the product is working as designed.

Get out of jail free

If you think that saying no is satisfying, and I most certainly do, being able to wash your hands of all responsibility by simply asserting that all is correct as far as you're concerned is just plain joyous. One simple statement and you are completely and utterly absolved of any guilt.

This might sound like a somewhat facile response and not in the spirit of helping your customers, but it's important to stick to your guns. You're going to have enough to fix as it is without having to take the time to address every wrinkle that someone doesn't like, and as I said before, there'll be plenty of people with a negative opinion.

So, enjoy your Get Out of Jail Free card. Just document the behaviour you consider to be right and then point all subsequent reports at your newly informative documentation and get on with your life.

Bugs aren't all bad

It's odd to think that we pay software developers hundreds of dollars a day to get things wrong, but that's the reality of software development, and it's been that way since day one.

You may recall an earlier quote from computing pioneer Sir Maurice Wilkes who said, 'As soon as we started programming, we found to our surprise that it wasn't as easy to get programs right as we had thought.' He went on to say, 'Debugging had to be discovered. I can remember the exact instant when I realized that a large part of my life from then on was going to be spent finding mistakes in my own programs.'

Yep.

You may have just put two and two together and realised that a sizable portion of your development budget is used to pay people to spend many hours making mistakes they can then spend even longer finding and then subsequently fixing. It's a horrible truth, but that's just how it is.

But, as grim as that may be, such things are all part of life's rich pageant, and it's why we construct large test environments to put candidate software through its paces on a regular basis. How many tests and how often they're run depends on who you are, the quality of your team and so on. Some are piecemeal, and let's just say, less than rigorous, while others have taken it to the other extreme with hundreds of thousands of tests running multiple times a day.

Sadly, there's no foolproof way of avoiding a few of your failures slipping through the net, so it's inevitable that your customers will come face to face with your fallibility. But while you may think this is a bad thing, this bit of the cloud definitely has a silver lining.

You see, it turns out that customers for the most part are quite forgiving. Provided your platform delivers the value it's supposed to and doesn't cause them excessive angst in the process, a bit of misbehaving UI and the occasional crash is really no problem. In fact, in some ways, they're not bad at all. I might even go as far as to call them good.

Bugs are inevitable and you will get knocked down. How you get up again will define you.

So when a customer reports a bug, even a major one, don't think of it as a crisis. Instead, embrace the opportunity to connect with your people and to deliver exemplary service.

If it's a showstopper, get the problem resolved as quickly as possible. If it's not, help them find a workaround and let them know when it's likely to be resolved. And when you do fix it, be sure to tell them.

Basically, do whatever you can to show that you care for their contin-ued patronage.

As I've said before, this is all about playing the long game, and building long-lasting relationships where you continue to help your people when they need it will do you no harm at all.

> **Top SaaS tip: A professionally managed bug is relationship gold.**

I want doesn't get

Showstopper issues must be dealt with quickly, but not all major bugs demand such close attention. Many can simply be added to the list and dealt with in the fullness of time, remembering of course that you should be investing in quality. It pays then to address them sooner rather than later.

Sadly though, your customers may not see things through the same lens, and you may well face demands for an immediate fix.

Such situations bring into focus your customers' likely ignorance with regards to your processes and the time it takes to get something done. They'll likely have little awareness that reproducing a bug can take time, discovering the root cause longer still, and even though the fix itself may literally require only a one-line change, it still has to be thoroughly tested.

This is critically important. While at an enterprise client of mine, I discovered that 5% of all bugs were created when fixing prior bugs.

Getting the customer moving is the most important outcome, so workarounds and mitigation techniques are the way forward. Annoyingly though, there are some who'd rather spit the dummy than search for a pragmatic solution, but I guess you can't help those who won't help themselves.

Compatibility

Change is the inevitable outcome of software ownership, and even if you never change a line of code after release, the technologies used to deliver it such as the browser most certainly will. You might be happy for a brief moment, but the combined juggernaut of your customers' needs and technology will continue on its merry way. Standing in front of it and hoping it will swerve will produce very predictable results.

Backward

The inevitability of mistakes, whether bugs or design issues, will give you plenty to ponder, and on top of that you're going to want to enhance and augment your offering. When you start to deliver this, you have the spectre of backward compatibility to manage.

This is simply the idea that everything you've made before must keep working. This doesn't mean you can't change what you've made though. Remember, your customers are paying for value and an outcome. Provided you still deliver both of those, how you do it can be open to interpretation, and as you're the one driving the car the choice of direction is yours.

You can then change the appearance or functional flow of your product. You can change where things appear, how they work and so much more. Provided the customer can still do what they've always done, you'll be just fine. This is not to suggest for a moment that you won't get to hear about any changes you might make, just that it'll generally be a storm in a teacup.

Forward

While you have a quite reasonable need to ensure that the past continues to be supported and that the wheels don't fall off whenever there's a change, you also have the future to contend with, and you'll be pleased to know it's out to get you.

If you're a fortune teller, the world's most prescient futurist or perhaps a deity of some kind, you'll doubtless have foreseen all that's to come and you can build your platform safe in the knowledge that you have all future bases covered. If you're human and annoyingly fallible like the rest of us, you'll just have to manage your problems as they come along.

Building forward compatibility into your product means that it will be able to cope with as yet unknown future input of some type, but this is somewhat tricky if you don't know what the future holds.

And I'm sure you won't be surprised to hear that the longer you own some software, the more likely it is that the future will be unkind.

Practically speaking, future compatibility problems, where your designs of the past are found to be wanting, are best met with the pragmatic realisation that all that lies ahead is far more valuable than all that's gone before. If the new stuff you want to add simply doesn't fit, so be it. You can park what you have and look for ways to help your people transition to the new variant.

Extensibility

The good news is that we in the IT industry learn from our mistakes – eventually. What we've discovered is that there are some good techniques that allow us to break the shackles of the past, provided we recognised in the past that in the future we'd need to break them.

Extensible designs, though typically far from perfect, usually allow for future changes to be managed far more elegantly and with minimal impact on all that's gone before. The good news is that your tech team should manage this for you, but it's a subject worth understanding just a little.

Versions

As you begin to enhance your product, you're going to add new features, fix bugs and so on. In the past, this would lead to multiple versions of a product existing because there was no practical way of forcing customers to upgrade to the next one. In the modern, connected internet world this is far easier to manage because what the user sees in their browser is whatever is delivered by you.

Happy days.

However, not all customers will necessarily want exactly the same features and functionality, and of course this is particularly pertinent in the business-to-business space because no two businesses are the same. The likely outcome here is that you'll get requests for features and occasionally asked for a special version, just for them.

Special versions

A classic scenario here sees the salesperson charging into the boss's office. She has the best, most super-duper prospect ever and wants you to make a special version of your platform, just for them. All you have to do is to agree and they'll buy your product, and to sweeten the deal they'll pay for all your development, testing and delivery costs.

So, all's good and you should get on with it, right?

Well … not so fast.

Firstly, there'll need to be some rather rigorous planning and the creation of a very precise specification. You'll likely need more complex contracts as well, just to make sure you're both protected in the event of difficulties.

This is going to make it far more time consuming to get the deal over the line, and as a result your cost of sale will go up significantly. While that's a touch inconvenient and something best avoided, for a big customer it might appear to be well worth the effort.

However, when you start to consider your cost of ownership, you may think differently.

The moment you create a second version, two things happen. The first is that you have two versions to maintain. This doesn't double your costs, but it will increase them. More importantly, you've drawn a new line in the sand and set a precedent.

So, what happens when the next super-duper prospect comes along wanting their own version and yet more changes?

You rinse and repeat.

So now you have three versions, then four, five and so on.

That's more complication, more code, more testing, more bugs, more help, more documentation, more training and, well, more everything. Your new clients may well be paying for all of the special stuff, the consultancy dollars might be spinning in your eyes with cartoonish enthusiasm and kerr-ching may be your new favourite word, but you're going to have to find all the resources to deliver the many variants and that's going to be a challenge to say the least.

It's guaranteed to take your focus too.

Perhaps more notably, you're effectively embracing a new business model. You're no longer selling a single SaaS solution, instead you're drifting closer to being a bespoke software consultancy. There's nothing inherently wrong with this, but as you'll see when we look at scaling it's a world that has its own set of challenges.

While you're trying to wrangle all of that, there's still a need to enhance your core platform. Will all the custom versions you've created be able to support the addition of the many features you want to add? If it can't, the complexity is going to get out of hand very quickly.

In effect, by trying to please everyone, you've created a very expensive and complex world, and all in all it's a situation best avoided if possible.

One size fits all

Back in chapter four, I argued that different users required different functionality. I will do no such thing here when talking about different customers though.

Having a single version of your reality is the choice of champions.

So, when asked for a special version the answer should always be no, with a but. Ignoring the wild nonsensical wants that often come with such requests, it's highly likely that many of the suggestions are perfectly reasonable and will add value not only for the super-duper prospect but also for the rest of your clients. So, you can offer to incorporate them into the product as part of the deal. Items that are 'must haves' can be prioritised and less pressing needs can be delivered over time. This may slow things down a little as you work how to deliver everything that's required, but it's a win–win.

You solve the client's problems and in return they help to solve some of yours, and a long-lasting, mutually beneficial partnership has begun.

I'm sure I've mentioned the importance of playing the long game once or twice before.

COST OF OWNERSHIP

As you're probably beginning to realise, the cost of getting to market is nothing compared to how much you're going to haemorrhage once you get there. If you haven't, now's a really good time for the penny to drop.

As I wrote previously, one of the major reasons so many SaaS businesses fail is that they simply run out of cash. Far too many entrepreneurs fail to grasp just how much money they're going to need to not only get the ball rolling, but also to ensure it doesn't stop when it hits a little incline.

Getting started is then the relatively easy part, and provided you have a big enough pile of cash you can build an MVP and take it to market. But you're now playing the long game, so when you're planning your budget and where you're going to spend your investment capital, you need to consider what's going to happen on the other side of your go-live date.

And the most notable thing about that is it's going to go on for far longer than the time it took you to build your MVP.

The day after

Going live and hitting the market is a cause for celebration, but in the cold light of dawn with your self-induced headache banging away, you'll realise that nothing much has changed. In fact, it will be much like the day before. It's nice to think that you might wake up to find you're about to be mown down by an invading horde of paying punters, but that's unlikely. You'll get some of course, and they'll undoubtedly generate some income, but until you've got quite a few on board it's going to be far more of a trickle than a flood.

This is why you need to keep your MVP super simple and get to market as quickly as possible.

You're going to be burning through cash for quite a while afterwards. You'll be paying for marketing campaigns to help get the word out there, and I'm sure you're going to need to eat something from time to time. You'll probably want a roof over your head too, and you may have a partner and family who'll want to continue living in the manner to which they've become accustomed.

Most notably, you're also going to carry on paying for development. Your MVP is just the beginning, so if you've spent $250,000 to create that, you can easily expect to spend at least that much again over the next 12 months, and likely a fair bit more. And as discussed previously, it's not like putting goods on the shelf of a store. Payback in the SaaS world is often a slow affair.

And if all of that isn't sobering enough, while you're hacking your way through the technology, you'll also have your new customers knocking on the door demanding yet more training, documentation and support, and you're going to be hard pressed to do all of that. So, you're going to need some help, and that's yet more money going out the door.

What's next

What's next is day two, then three, then four, then ...., and the realisation that all of the above are really just part of life's rich pageant and part and parcel of the wonderfully exciting and utterly petrifying software world. Still, c'est la vie.

TECHNICAL DEBT

I know, I know. I paint a bleak picture and it can't really be all that bad … can it?

It can, you know. The cautionary tales I've shared are just some that I know about, and there are many more out there just waiting to be told.

Still, you've gotta be in it to win it.

As your team is ploughing through its many challenges, design mistakes, bugs and the like are inevitable. So is compromise. You and they will be faced with problems, and circumstances will likely dictate that you can't always apply your preferred level of diligence and rigour.

When this happens, quality will be replaced by expediency, and you'll knowingly create your first bit of technical debt, which is the price you'll pay tomorrow to fix up whatever you couldn't get right yesterday and today. What really sucks is that some of it won't be your fault. You might rely on a third-party solution at some point and then you'll have to deal with whatever slings and arrows they throw your way.

Mitigation

So, developers get things wrong, necessity is the mother of some horrible invention, and life gives you lemons. Software ownership can be a little unkind from time to time.

At least it's nothing personal.

For SaaS and business leaders alike, technical debt, like its financial cousin, is all too easy to get in to, and you always end up paying back more than you borrowed. Happily, forewarned is still forearmed, and for those yet to get too deep in the proverbial, there's still a chance to mitigate as much of the potential damage as possible.

Of course, if you're already waist deep in the brown stuff, there's a strong chance that when you do find your feet, they may no longer be in your wellies and dragging yourself out will be a slow and mucky business. Whatever the root cause of your debt, beware the temptation to throw yet more time and money at working around the problem. It's rarely the right answer. Best of course is to find the root cause and to solve for that.

Some debt is good

As you're playing the long game, prior investments in relatively poor outcomes are simply sunk costs. They're the tolls and parking tickets you pay along your way as you head towards your bright and shiny SaaS future. However, you can only spend your resources once, and while it's best to do it wisely, knowing what to do is hard. You can pay off your debt today and tidy up your mess, or you can accept your fate and invest in tomorrow knowing that it comes with a greater cost.

The question as ever is whether now is the right time to repay some of the debt. Which option is right for you will of course depend on your circumstances.

The good news is that debt, whether financial or technical, isn't necessarily bad. Like many businesses, having a financial debt in the short to medium term can be a useful facility that enables business development, gets tools to market and more. It's a means to an end, just as your mortgage lets you live in a nicer house than you otherwise would be able to afford.

Technical debt is no different. You just need to ensure that the cost of owning it doesn't get out of hand.

ADAPTABILITY

Early decisions will come with some debt. It's all but inevitable. It may even be insurmountable or simply uneconomical to consider changing.

Still, all is not lost.

Instagram, as you may recall, pivoted early in its existence, leveraging a picture-sharing feature on its hotel booking platform to create a new offering. This is the essence of adaptability, and it puts me in mind of Charles Darwin and evolution. The animal kingdom is littered with species that started out one way and ended up very different indeed. Human embryos for example have structures that look very much like gill slits, although they go on to become parts of the ear and jaw.

So, as I'm one for looking at everything other than the technology, I wondered what lessons there might be for SaaS entrepreneurs in this evolutionary model, and then one day I had a chat with a couple of fintech business leaders.

The gentlemen in question have a platform that uses AI and machine learning. It does all sorts of automated activities, managing investment portfolios, buying here, selling there and generally improving the user's wealth. It's clever stuff without a doubt, but while it might be considered to be a cutting-edge offering, you probably won't be surprised to find out that like so many SaaS platforms, they have plenty of competition. They may be jumping on the bandwagon, but just a few years ago someone was first to offer a product in this space. They would have looked at the results people could achieve, applied early versions of AI and machine learning, demonstrated their superiority over their pitiful human rivals, and romped off to colonise an untapped market.

When it comes to selling human technology advancements, and SaaS platforms in particular, being able to offer a fractional improvement over the competition ain't all that.

Offer us a 20% return and we're listening. Offer us 1% and … you know … not so much. However, unlike nature's unguided process of evolution, we can strategise. We can predict the future too, and for new innovations and things like AI and machine learning there's one very definite eventuality ahead.

Our gains will diminish over time.

When we use the latest technologies, we know that our early gains will be massive, but they will give way to smaller and smaller improvements until we come up with the next generation. AI might seemingly be charging ahead right now, but the next really big leap won't come along until the arrival of quantum computing, and that won't be ready to join the mainstream for some time.

Survival

So, what should a SaaS business do until the next big thing arrives? Well, there are a couple of options.

The first is that you continue to focus on the evolutionary arms race in the hope that you can outrun the competition and grab the lion's share, and if not that, at least a considerable portion of the market.

The alternative is that you move your focus elsewhere. You continue to build on your skills, but rather than focusing on the technology, you wrap them up in a new offering that delivers new value to a new niche where the initial massive gains made with the technology are yet to be fully realised.

Which is the better choice will of course depend on you and your market, but as Darwin never actually said, 'It is not the strongest of the species that survives, not the most intelligent. It is the one that is the most adaptable to change.'

TRUST

AI keeps popping up as a subject and whenever it does, trust – or perhaps distrust – is never far behind, and it's something that all software vendors large and small need to be on top of.

Trust, it turns out, is very much like a soap bubble. All it takes is one careless prick and it's gone for ever. This may be a coarse bit of humour from my school days, but the sentiment is nonetheless accurate. One teensy, weensy, tiny little abuse of your position and things will never be the same again.

Prospects, customers and the many other people you deal with will assume that you're trustworthy. They'll assume you'll do the right thing and look after them. You can make mistakes, provided you make amends for them, but if you abuse the relationship in anyway the bond will be broken and regaining their trust will be all but impossible.

Understanding this is of paramount importance. Your future quite literally depends on it.

Let's say you have a data breach – and in Australia roughly 30% of those are caused by human error – you're going to have some adverse publicity, but that may be the least of your problems. IBM figures suggest that an average event will cost a business nearly $4.5 million dollars and may result in customer churn of over 20%.

Those are business-killing figures.

Of course, you have to land the customers first, and there's an ongoing battle between our desire for convenience and our trust of a vendor. High profile cases like Facebook's engagement with the now defunct Cambridge Analytica have done little to help, bringing data use and trust very much into the mainstream news cycle. Definitive figures are hard to come by, but anecdotally the majority believe that trust is more important than convenience and most would rather use a different service if they thought that their privacy wasn't being protected. Nearly 60% of people are believed to have put this opinion into practice.

So, for SaaS vendors, the trust component is critical.

Yet another cautionary tale

To help you understand the effect that a lack of trust can have, we need look no further than the Australian Government's CovidSafe app.

This was made available in the relatively early days of 2020 as we all began to wrestle with our new pandemic normal. It worked by monitoring the local area for other people with the app running on their device. If the two remained together for a prescribed amount of time, the association was recorded so that authorities could trace individuals in the event of one of them testing positive.

The application stored data centrally, though why this model was chosen is unclear. Alternative solutions were available that would have ensured complete anonymity for users. Still, early download numbers suggested the app would help the cause, with millions of people installing it. However, from the get-go there were concerns among many that the data would be used by law enforcement or for other governmental purposes, despite assurances that it was only an emergency public health measure. Government trust was running at around 33% at the time, and this did little to ease concerns.

Singapore had built an equivalent app and the government there is trusted to a far greater extent. But even their roughly 67% trust could only equate to around a quarter of the population installing the app.

It soon became apparent that Australian law enforcement was indeed trying to access the data and what vestige of trust remained was soon gone.

Ultimately CovidSafe was a $21 million failure that made little to no contribution to contact tracing. That many refused to install it for fear of government overreach was a significant contributory factor in this.

Privacy practices

It wasn't so long ago that the public rarely gave much thought to the ethical use of data. Then the aforementioned Cambridge Analytica arrived on the scene and as ever it all kicked off the moment someone's metaphorical beer got spilled. In this case it was the harvesting of the personal data of 87 million people by an organisation that was in the business of trying to affect election outcomes.

Ethical standards, once thought perhaps optional, are now de rigueur, and every business, whether a SaaS vendor or not, should have privacy as a fundamental tenet of their existence.

Should your own sense of propriety not be quite enough to focus your attention or keep you on the straight and narrow here, I'll casually remind you that there are some hefty penalties available for businesses that don't do the right thing. In Australia, for example, breaches of the privacy law can attract fines of the greater of up to $10 million or three times any benefit obtained from the invasion breach, and 10% of Australian annual revenue.

And if you're going to do business in Europe, there's GDPR (General Data Protection Regulation) to contend with, and the Europeans ain't messing about. Their fines extend to €20 million and 4% of global turnover.

In short, privacy is a monster and I strongly recommend that you perform an annual privacy review to ensure you're doing the right thing. There are specialist businesses in this space that can help.

Seven privacy principles

While you're waiting for your privacy expert to get back to you to arrange a visit, here are seven privacy principles for you to digest:

- **Proactive not reactive, preventative not remedial.** Don't wait for it all to go wrong and then try to fix it. Take the time and effort to assess potential risks and prevent breaches long before they have a chance to occur. This applies to you, your team and anyone else entrusted with your data.

- **Privacy as a default setting.** Always, and without fail, protect personal information, whether that's within your product or your business. If you're not sure whether a piece of data is private, assume that it is.

- **Privacy embedded into design.** Privacy should be at the forefront of your design, whether that's platform features, services or anything else.

- **Full functionality: positive-sum not zero-sum.** Privacy works for both you and your people. You should think of everything to do with privacy as a need and a win–win rather than an either/or. Privacy and security are not interchangeable.

- **End-to-end security – full lifecycle protection.** Without security there is no privacy. Be sure to implement robust security measures and destroy all data once it has served its purpose.

- **Visibility and transparency – keep it open.** Be honest and up front. Tell your customers precisely what data you're collecting, why you're doing and it and how you're going to manage it. Best is to create a robust privacy policy document. A privacy specialist will help you get this right.

- **Respect for user privacy – keep it user-centric.** If you're looking at the technology, you're missing the point. Put the interests of your many people at the centre of your designs and plans, and be sure to keep them informed in an appropriate manner whenever there's a need. If you're not sure whether someone needs to know, they probably do.

Top SaaS tip: Treat their data as you would your own passwords.

Security

Your systems can be hacked, no matter how strong you think the security. This is not hyperbole, scaremongering or me trying to sell you a cybersecurity audit or insurance, though both are a great idea.

It's an objective and unequivocal fact.

As an industry, we've come a long way in the last two decades. The internet is a far more secure space than it ever has been, company networks are stronger too, and even retail and home network routers now use encrypted traffic by default. Sadly though, they're all still incredibly flawed and are increasingly being affected by the profusion of IoT (internet of things) devices being attached to networks.

I have a washing machine on my network, and I have no idea whether it's using the most up-to-date security protocols or not, nor whether the manufacturer updates its firmware if they find a loophole. The big question of course is whether they're actually looking for such things in the first place or simply responding to a problem when they get round to it.

After all, they sell household electrical devices, so it's hard to believe wireless network security is uppermost on their agenda.

It is for the many people who make a living by breaching security though, and they're very good at it. In fact, the best are well-organised professionals who make a motza breaking into corporate networks to extort money from unsuspecting business owners.

And the bigger you are, the more attractive you are as a target.

Logistics and freight forwarding business Expeditors International, with revenues of around $10 billion, were affected in early 2022 and it played havoc, forcing them to shut down their operations for a while.

Security, just like privacy, is a specialist space and I once more urge you to undertake a comprehensive security review every year and to make it a core component of your platform and your business practices.

Failure

Since 2018, Facebook, LinkedIn, Marriott International, Alibaba, Accenture and many more have been breached in some way. Facebook, again, neglected its obligations and didn't mention its breach for two years, a decision that ultimately cost it $5 billion. As noted previously, the fines for the release of private data are severe and you'd be well advised to undertake further research around your obligations under the *Privacy Act 1988* and your responsibilities with regards to notifiable data breaches.

Whether any SaaS vendors have gone out of business specifically because of a cybersecurity issue is unclear, though doubtless a bit of diligent research will turn up a case or two. It's certainly been reported that a large number of small and medium-sized businesses have been grossly affected, and are in fact the primary target of cybercrime because they're relatively easy pickings.

Given that failure is very much an option, you'd be somewhat cavalier to charge ahead without some robust policies in place to ensure that when your security is breached you're not only in a position to get back up again but also to report the incident to the appropriate authorities. Your tech team should of course be all over this, but as ever forewarned is forearmed and you need to be on top of the fundamentals of security both within your application and your business in general.

Eight tips for application security

The internet is awash with tips and techniques about security within a business, and as ever I encourage you to find out more. However, there's not so much with regards to the kind of access control and security your platform should offer, so here's a few high-level pointers.

- **Least privilege.** Ensure that every feature is subject to a security check and that the default is no, regardless of who the user is. If you stick to this simple principle, your chance of creating a loophole is greatly reduced.
- **Separation of duties.** Try to avoid any one person having access to vast swathes of the application. Specific user roles come in

handy here. The finance team may need access to the accounting functionality, but they won't need access to HR.

- **Obscurity is not security.** You may have ways of directly accessing features, perhaps via a specific URL and only you and the team may know them. Hoping they'll stay hidden is not a security policy.

- **Defence in depth.** Multiple layers of security increase your chance of success. Users need to be verified to sign in and may need further verification to access the data tables associated with a feature. The cost of checking authorities is minimal. The cost of dealing with a breach isn't.

- **Fail securely.** If your application is going to fail, and it will, ensure if fails in an organised manner. Every potential failure point, and that's just about every request that goes to your webserver, needs to be completely protected.

- **Trust no one.** Your application will almost certainly use third-party functionality and features. You should assume that everyone else is a basket case and likely to bring your world crashing down, so check everything they do and give them the least level of privilege necessary.

- **Keep it simple.** There's no reason to make application and user security complex. It can all be managed with a simple architecture that repeatedly asks who you are and what you are trying to do.

- **Be a small target.** When it comes to security, less is very much more. The less you expose to the outside world, the more likely it is that bad people will be kept at a safe distance.

My own personal approach to security is adequately described by this next top tip.

Top SaaS tip: The answer's no! What's the question?

GROWING AND SCALING

Getting to market, finding customers and planning your assault on the remainder of the mountain you're yet to climb comes with a great sense of satisfaction and rather a lot of trepidation too. There is much to be done if you're to take your burgeoning empire to the next level.

More of everything

To grow and scale your business, you're going to need more of just about everything, and then you're going to need to fill in the gaps. You can think of this a bit like the spokes on a wheel. At the centre they're all close together but as they extend further out, the gaps between them start to widen. Activities that seem quite simple when you're a small team just get so much bigger and consuming when you scale.

New people

Let's say you're beginning to build your internal development team and you're going to employ one new developer. First there's the hiring process. You can probably manage that with an ad and interview process, and you can go out and buy a new laptop before they start. When they do, the existing team can onboard them and help get them up to speed.

If you're doing well you might start to hire more, perhaps one a month. One was okay, but repeating this every month takes a fair bit of effort across the board. You might outsource some work to a recruiter or hire someone else to manage the process. As the numbers grow, so does the complication, and it's not long before you want to systemise as much as possible, investing in quality as you go.

This too takes resources.

By the time you get to three or four a month, you need a team dedicated to talent acquisition and onboarding. Your tech inventory is growing quickly too, so you'll need to scale the technical team as well. While all that's going on, business is booming, so the support team has to grow, as does client onboarding, education, evangelists and so on.

In short, scaling demands people – and a lot of them. And the more you have, the more you need.

Too many people

More people means a bigger wage bill, and that's great if you're selling more and revenues are increasing. But what happens if the market flattens or, as has happened recently, interest rates rise and investors are less keen to supply the cash to feed your voracious appetite?

Ignoring the worst-case scenario of going out of business, you'll need to find ways to cut your spending. But where to cut is rarely clear.

You need all your support and customer-facing people, and if you get rid of some of them you'll be behind the eight ball if the market picks up again. You also risk reputational damage if you can't deliver what's been promised, so you're pretty much stuck having to pay the wage of a bunch of people who are 'on the beach' as we used to call consultants with no direct customer work.

You could make some developers redundant, but that's always a last resort, is rarely good for public opinion, and feels like a bit of a false economy. And as before, the moment the cash situation improves, you'll have to waste valuable resources finding replacements.

All things considered, you're stuck between a rock and a hard place ... again.

Offshore development

Finding cheaper resources in less expensive countries sounds like it might mitigate some of your development costs, but is it really cheaper? If you're looking solely at cash outlay, it probably is, though it's worth noting that it's far more expensive today than it was just a few years ago.

Remote teams are complex to manage too, despite the advances with international communication via Microsoft Teams, Zoom et al. Behaviour and practices are less opaque, and developer skills may be lower, reducing quality of code and increasing delivery time.

There can be language and communication issues, cultural differences, and subject matter expertise needs to be transferred too. Your logistics are subject to the tyranny of distance and time zones, and differing legal frameworks and professional ethics may mean your IP is not as secure as it was. And just for good measure, your onshore people are needed to educate and guide your remote team, reducing their productivity.

And before you think you can just get a few more cheaper people to solve the problem, Brook's Law suggests that adding people typically slows projects down.

It's little wonder then that some figures suggest that initial cost estimates of offshore development can rise by as much as two-thirds.

This is of course a somewhat bleak picture, and offshore development is increasingly being used to great effect. I've been involved with it myself and it's gone very well. However, we typically get what we pay for, and what we save in cash we often spend in other ways.

Partners

So, scaling on your own comes with a wide array of expensive problems that demand access to a steady supply of cash, and surprise, surprise, it's the many needs and wants of the myriad people involved that cause all the complications. Whether your business can sustain a full-service model where you provide all the human resources will depend entirely on what you do and how you do it, but there are risks involved and a need for significant liquidity just in case all doesn't go to plan.

If it does, you'll get paid very well, but if it doesn't, well, let's not think about that too much.

Do what you do best

Happily, there is an alternative.

Way back in chapter one I introduced my structured 4Ps framework, the last P of which was partners, and I wrote that they'd offer your business flexibility, fluidity and the chance to focus on what you do best.

Now is their moment to shine.

The full-service model, with the typically lucrative implementation, education and consulting fees, does sound tempting, but trying to keep all the pie to yourself could be construed as a little greedy.

But what if you share the wealth?

Investing in a distributed partner network makes scaling far simpler. You get to focus on delivering a high-quality product while they worry about managing all of the services. Not only that, they'll reduce your support costs and also help with a lot of sales legwork. They have to if they want more income month on month.

It's a team game

Better still, they take the strain when there's a shift in the market. If there's a spike in demand, it's no longer just you having to find resources. Instead, you can spread the load across your multiple distribution partners. If one doesn't have people available, it's likely that another one will.

Similarly, if there's a downturn, your partners are far better positioned to shoulder the additional burden because there's every chance they look after other products as well, and they'll be better able to absorb the impact.

So, rather than grabbing everything yourself, spread the love around a little. You'll make less in the good times but be far more protected when they're bad.

> **Top SaaS tip: Share the gain to reduce your pain.**

Going international

Now that the idea of partners is floating around you might be tempted to think about spreading your wings a little. You might even consider trying to conquer some far-off lands. And why not? Over half the world's population now has internet access, and I know from my work with Create Care Global that we're more likely to have access to a phone signal than sanitation.

Of the over five billion using the internet, around a quarter speak English as a first language, a massive proportion speak it as a second or third, and well over half of all websites are in English. If you're a SaaS vendor using English you have a global market just waiting for you to arrive. All you need then are a few ads in some appropriate jurisdictions and you're good to go … right?

Multilingual requirements

From a simplistic perspective, that's pretty much it, but as ever, there's a little more to consider, not least of which is that it's somewhat of an assumption that you'll get by with an English-only approach. After all, this is a website we're talking about, meaning you can't just speak loudly and slowly and stick an O on the end of a few nouns as the stereotypical British tourist in Spain is often portrayed as doing.

Even branching out to countries with a lot in common – such as the UK, US and Australia, depending on where you are reading this – requires subtle changes if you're going to be effective. Australia and the US use dollars while the UK uses pounds. The UK and US have differences in terms of spelling, and in the US, dates are formatted as month, day, year rather than day, month, year. These are perhaps not the most onerous of problems to solve, but it means you need variations for specific locales and these need to be baked into your platform.

And if you go further afield there's the many languages, which means you need to translate every piece of text on the screen, all help and documentation, training courses, add subtitles to videos and so on. This takes a lot of work, and while AI and natural language processing are coming along well, this is one time when relying on Google translate is a bad idea. It's good, but there are numerous examples of times when it's failed, particularly when you only have a few words and there is no context.

And as mentioned previously, mainland Europe also formats numbers differently, swapping commas and full stops. Instead of 1,234,567.89 it's 1.234.567,89.

For example, consider the word 'set'. It's the English word with the most meanings according to Guinness World Records, with at least 430 different senses in the *Oxford English Dictionary*. Unsurprisingly, 'set' also has the longest entry with some 60,000 words.

How many is that? Well, that's about as much as you've read in this book so far, depending on what swingeing cuts my beloved editor has made.

Legal stuff

I'm sure it goes without saying but operating in different countries means you're subject to a raft of different legislation. Not only is this codified in legal speak, which is hard enough to understand for many, it's also legalese in a different language which is a double whammy.

Worse still, legal statutes change regularly, and keeping up with them requires significant effort. Australia's WiseTech Global offers the CargoWise platform, helping businesses move their stuff around the planet. It has teams dotted around the world to ensure local legislation requirements are properly adhered to.

Unsurprisingly, I strongly recommend that you obtain some very thorough legal advice.

Pricing issues

Currency fluctuations mean that you may have to offer a different price depending on where you are in the world, but local market conditions will have an effect too. At the time of writing, HubSpot charges €41 per month for one of its offerings in Europe, and $45 in Australia, yet the exchange rate is roughly $1.50 per Euro.

Step by step

Throw in a few cultural differences just to muddy the waters even more, and I think you'll agree that attacking a new market is no walk in the park. In fact, it all takes a lot of time, effort and money to get right, and your cost of ownership just goes up and up. So, unless you're swimming in investment capital and liquidity, adding a new locale to your venture tends to stretch your market and development resources very thinly.

I've been asked to help launch at least ten different products in Australia, and for some reason they always offer me a percentage of revenue as a reward.

I could be tempted if they were a leader in their market, but none have ever been in the top ten and I'm yet to say yes. The reason for this is simple. Going global requires traction in each location, with word of mouth, referrals and a solid customer lifetime value. It requires that you know your market intimately.

But if you're not winning where you are, why would a new market fix everything for you?

You can pivot and take on a new location, but doubling down is a very risky strategy, and as a general rule it's far better to be winning in one than being mediocre in many.

MEASURING EVERYTHING

However your venture works out, it's going to be a hell of a journey, and it's probably best that you keep a record of what's happened and what's happening as you go along. Data is after all the new gold, and even if you don't know what to do with it today, recording it means you can at least look at it later. With that in mind, I started to collate a few of the metrics you should probably keep a good eye on.

As ever, Google is awash with opinion on this topic and when I searched for others' thoughts on what to measure, I was rewarded with 34,000,000 pages. Luckily, the first few dozen that I skimmed through had some regular themes, so creating a list is no great challenge. However, most notably, nearly all the metrics listed relate to customer acquisition, sales, retention, churn, EBITDA and so on. Few had any reference whatsoever to the production side of SaaS and being a software creator.

Knowing how your sales and customer numbers are tracking is without doubt something you should all be on top of, but paying scant regard to the vast piles of cash you'll burn creating and delivering your masterpiece is asking for trouble. Your primary outlay will be wages, and with a decent Australian developer costing in the region of $10,000 per month, getting anything done is going to be expensive. It's probably wise then to record lots of data about your development practices as well.

So, here are just a few of the many metrics that you might like to record, and as management consultant Peter Drucker is alleged to said, 'If you can't measure it, you can't manage it.' He never did say that, but the idea is still a good one.

Development

Given how much you're going to spend on your developers and testers, knowing how they spend their time is invaluable.

Check-ins

A count of the number of times code is committed to your source repository.

As a general rule, code is checked in when a task is completed. However, should it fail a test, it may need to be modified and checked in again, and again. The higher the average number of check-ins per task, the lower the quality of what's being submitted.

Source management tools such as GitHub have many relevant metrics available.

Code

Knowing the volume of code, modules, source files and more gives a sense of the size of an application and its growth over time.

However, you can't use the volume of code as a measure of productivity. I've seen developers spend a day working on a defect only to write one or two lines to fix it once they understood the root cause. Similarly, I've seen developers hammering out hundreds of lines a day, with much copied and modified from existing source.

Cycle time

This is the amount of time taken to complete a task from go to whoa, not the hours spent working on it.

Thus, a task worked on for an hour on Monday morning and then another hour to complete it on Tuesday afternoon would have roughly 16 hours cycle time but only have a task time of two hours.

Cycle times give an important insight into the smoothness and quality of your processes. As a rule of thumb, the more focused your team is, the less task switching and the higher the quality of their work, the shorter the cycle time will be.

Defect lead time

An estimate of the amount of time required to resolve all existing defects.

If you're fixing defects as a priority, this number will indicate how much work there is to complete before you can work on new projects and features.

Defects after release

A count of the number of defects detected after the product has been tested.

Higher numbers suggest strongly that your testing regime doesn't have the quality and coverage that it should.

Defects during testing

A count of the number of defects detected while your product is being tested.

Higher numbers suggest strongly that your development quality has room for improvement. Lower numbers may mean a higher quality but may also suggest that there aren't enough tests being created.

Defects completed

The number of defects rectified as a percentage of the overall outstanding defect count.

Higher numbers suggest that you're addressing the bulk of the defects that you know of.

Developer head count

The total number of developers working on a product.

This is a critical metric to maintain. As the team grows so will many metrics like the number of defects or the lines of code. It's important then to normalise your metrics based on the number of people involved.

Task time

The number of hours spent working directly on a task.

Thus, a task worked on for an hour on Monday morning and then another hour to complete it on Tuesday afternoon would have roughly 16 hours cycle time but only have a task time of two hours.

Task time gives a sense of how big individual work activities are. A task time and cycle time that are closely related suggests that your team is able to focus on the job at hand.

Tasks completed

The number of individual tasks completed in a given time.

Tasks completed gives a sense of the throughput of the team, although this can be affected by the nature of the tasks and the time taken to complete individual activities.

It's important to normalise task-related metrics based on the developer head count.

Tasks in progress

The number of tasks currently being worked on by the team.

Smaller numbers suggest that the team is focused on the job at hand rather than being distracted by multiple concurrent activities.

Tasks outstanding

A count of the number of tasks currently recorded and planned for development.

You may wish to count pending tasks and work you might want to do one day, but if they're not yet on the radar for development they're of little value.

Test coverage

The percentage of your application currently under automated testing.

This is a rough measure that can be evaluated based on functionality and the many features of your product, or perhaps by using an average number of lines of code covered by a test. However you do it, the higher the number the better. There are few occasions when the phrase 'too many tests' has any real value.

Test runs

The number of times a day that your tests or a subset of them are executed.

In continuous integration and deployment environments, tests are often run for small sections of the code as they're submitted. Knowing which areas are being tested and how often will allow you to further optimise your processes.

Test failures

The number of tests that failed when testing a change to the source code.

Higher numbers suggest a lower quality of code being submitted. Lower numbers suggest a better quality, but it may also be that there is insufficient test coverage in that area.

Sales and marketing metrics

All the money being spent on going to market needs to generate some interest. The more you can find out about your processes and the results they generate the better.

Demo to conversion rate

How many demonstrations result in a paying customer?

Lead to conversion rate

How many leads turning into a paying customer?

You can further dissect all lead data into conversion rates for marketing-qualified leads (MQL), product-qualified leads (PQL) and sales-qualified leads (SQL).

Lead to free conversion rate

How many leads turn into a non-paying customer?

Lead to demonstration rate

How many leads are converted into a demonstration?

Marketing-qualified leads

How many leads have engaged with your marketing content or connected with your marketing team in some way?

Net promoter score

Ask your customers to rate how likely they are to recommend your solution on a scale from one to ten. Promoters will score nine or ten, neutrals seven or eight, and everyone else is a detractor. Then subtract the percentage of detractors from the percentage of promoters – that's your NPS.

$$NPS = Promoter\ \% - Detractor\ \%$$

This gives you an insight into how satisfied your customers are. Asking additional qualitative questions like why they rated you that way can help provide a better understanding.

New users

A super-simple measure of the number of signups each month.

Product-qualified leads

How many leads have engaged with your product, perhaps by using a free version or seeing a demonstration.

Referrals

How many leads are being generated by your existing customer base?

It's a rough rule, but if your referrals are increasing, it's a fair sign you're doing something right.

Sales-qualified leads

The number of leads who've been vetted by the sales team and are ready to be moved into your sales process.

Social media engagement

Content marketing is very much in vogue and it's important to track the performance of your posts, including the number of views, reactions, shares and whatever is available on the particular channel. These will likely change depending on whether it's a video, image and text, link to an article and so on.

Unique visitors

Whether you measure this weekly or monthly, it gives you a good sense of the size of your audience and how much engagement your marketing is attracting.

Customer and revenue metrics

You've spent a heap of time and money landing customers, so it's best to learn as much as you can about them and how they contribute towards your bottom line.

Annual recurring revenue

A simple measure of how much revenue your customers generate every year, typically derived by multiplying the monthly recurring revenue by twelve.

Active users

Having lots of users is great. Having lots that are actively using your platform is even better.

Average revenue per customer

Divide your monthly recurring revenue by the number of customers.

This is not the most important metric to track, but it will give you a sense of how much a typical customer generates each month.

Churn rate

When a customer stops being a customer they've churned. This is one of the more important metrics, particularly in high-volume businesses.

A churn rate of 2% per month means you're losing a quarter of your customers every year, and as it's somewhere between five and twenty-five times more expensive to find a new customer than it is to keep an existing one, you'd be wise to keep your churn rate to a minimum.

Customer acquisition cost

Knowing how much it costs to get your customers on board is important. Without this simple bit of knowledge, you're at risk of grossly affecting your profitability.

Happily, working out the cost of getting a customer on board is fairly straightforward. You just add up all the money you've spent on marketing, sales, wages and so on and divide that by the number of customers you've acquired.

Customer lifetime value

The revenue generated by an average customer over their lifetime using your product, and unsurprisingly bigger is definitely better. Combined with additional information about the source of the customer, this is critical to helping you understand what strategies are the most profitable and where best to focus your marketing budget.

Lifetime value is typically compared to customer acquisition cost. A ratio of 3:1 is often considered to be the minimum for a SaaS business, although I've seen it suggested that 6:1 should be your aim. Whichever it is, the bigger the ratio, the better.

Customer retention rate

On the flipside to churn rate is retention rate. Retaining customers is a no brainer. The more you keep the better life will be.

Customer satisfaction

Knowing how happy your customers are is one of your key metrics. Net Promoter Score is sometimes used as a guide for satisfaction, but you can also monitor sentiment in social media mentions, live chat, follow-up surveys and more.

The more you engage with your community, the better the chance of getting a good result.

Freemium to paid conversion

Having a freemium version of your platform to entice people in is great, but if they're not turning into paying punters, you're just giving your platform away for the fun of it.

There are many opinions as to what a good rate of conversion is, but 3% to 4% is a solid start.

Monthly recurring revenue

A simple measure of how much revenue your customers generate every month.

Return on investment

Knowing how much you're generating based on the money you're spending is one of the more important measures. A typical way of measuring ROI as a percentage is to divide your monthly recurring revenue by your costs.

$$ROI \% = (MRR \div Costs) \times 100$$

Users

A simple count of the number of people signed up to use your platform.

Upselling revenue

Just as referrals are an indicator of the quality of your product, so is your upselling revenue as customers move from a cheaper to a more expensive product. As they use more of your offering, they become more entwined.

An increase in upselling revenue suggests that you're delivering the kind of value your customers want.

Support metrics

Poor service standards can kill a SaaS business in truly short order, so find out all you can about how your team looks after your people.

Average first response time

The importance of the second S cannot be overstated, so be sure to keep an eye on how quickly your support team engages with the customer when there's a problem. Remember, this may be through multiple channels such as chat, email and phone, and each will have its own characteristics and expectations.

Average resolution time

Being quick to engage with the customer is good, but you also need to solve the problem, and the quicker the better. As with first response time, the various communication channels will present a different dynamic when dealing with the customer. Knowing which produces the best outcomes means you can direct them appropriately, depending on their issue.

Backlog

Having a sense of how many tickets are waiting for attention at any given moment will give you a better understanding of the customer's experience and provide a good insight into whether you have sufficient people available during busy periods.

Customer effort

This is a somewhat vague metric to help determine how long customers typically spend working to resolve their problem. You might measure this using a question about the ease of the experience, similar to a Net Promoter Score.

Customer satisfaction

There's no better time to deliver great service than when you're helping solve a customer's problem, so you might as well ask for some feedback about both their experience and the product while you're doing it.

Interactions per ticket

In a perfect world one interaction would be enough. However, your team will likely have multiple engagements before a ticket can be closed. While it is ideal to keep this number to a minimum, remember that every interaction is an opportunity to deliver exceptional service, even if it's managing the report of a defect.

Support tickets per customer

You might get a lot of tickets but then you might have a lot of customers. In a perfect world, this is a number that will get smaller and smaller as you invest more in documentation, training and the overall quality of your product.

Time per ticket

It may take several days to find a resolution, but it may only occupy the team for a few hours. Knowing how long an average ticket takes, particularly if it's related to certain aspects of your product, will help you allocate resources more accurately to ensure customers get the best outcomes.

Performance metrics

Knowing how performant your platform is allows you to plan for the future more effectively, ensuring your customers continue to receive a high-quality solution.

Availability

The percentage of time that your system is up and running versus the time that it's unavailable.

This is a simple aggregate measure that helps you understand the overall picture and how your customers will likely perceive your availability.

Your goal is of course to achieve the magical 100%.

Concurrent use

Knowing how many users are online and how many instances of your application exist at any given moment will help you understand how resources need to be allocated. This can also help you plan scheduled downtimes should the need arise.

Failure rate

A simple measure of the number of times your application fails, whether that's a crash, server problems, webserver issues or anything else.

There is a world of difference between a single failure for an hour and sixty individual one-minute outages, and they'll typically indicate very different types of issues.

Mean time between failures

Software systems fail from time to time and for a wide variety of reasons. This metric is the average time that your system remains upright.

Note that not all failures are the same and it's well worth distinguishing between the different types. The more you record about issues, the better chance you have of predicting the likelihood of an incident.

Mean time to recover

All systems will fall over at some point. The big question is how long it takes to get back up again. Mean time to recover is your average downtime.

Response time

How long does it take for your system to respond from the moment of request to the screen update completing?

Knowing the average is important, but knowing how each component part of your platform performs is more so.

Throughput

Just as we might measure the performance of a human worker based on items per hour or similar, we can do the same with software by measuring the number of transactions.

Response time is an end-to-end measure with several component pieces. Throughput is a simple assessment of how your platform performs once it's received a request.

How to measure everything

Here I am suggesting that you record enough data to keep yourself entertained for millennia, yet I've given you little to go on as to how to do it. And that's for good reason. My job is to raise your awareness of the many problems there are to be solved and to guide you towards a start point for solving them for yourself. Apart from that, it's simply impossible for me to recommend something when I don't know the very specific problems that you're trying to solve.

The software world, as you should understand by now, is incredibly specialised and you'll need to work with your technical teams to determine the right tools to use for the jobs at hand. The only problem is that there are literally thousands to choose from and their number changes with disturbing rapidity. This is unsurprising as many are SaaS businesses themselves and they're subject to the same problems that you face.

Happily, there are sites like Capterra.com that specialise in providing insights into the many offerings available, showing shortlists of the top players, emerging favourites and more. And it's a good job too. I put in 'testing' and received 24 categories of testing software. When I selected 'user testing' there were 49 products. There were over 100 performance testing tools and nearly 400 automated testing tools.

It's no wonder that so many specialists find their favourites and stick with them, and doubtless your team will do the same.

It may also be the case that some measurements need to be coded into your systems by your development team.

Averages vs distributions

Many of the metrics I've listed are averages that help you understand the general landscape. However, while such measures are undoubtedly useful, having a clear picture of the overall distribution of data is perhaps more so. This is particularly helpful when trying to understand the impact of data that is skewed or biased, or where there are significant outliers.

For example, you may have an average downtime of around one minute per day. However, that could be caused by a six-hour outage one day and perfection the rest, a one-second outage two or three times an hour, or a seven-minute outage every Friday lunchtime.

By monitoring the distribution of the events and data points, you'll get a far clearer understanding of the situation and they may well point to a regular issue that can be resolved, or at least mitigated.

The apocryphal tale of the system that inexplicably went down every evening because the cleaner was using the plug socket comes to mind.

SUMMARY

Is that the extent of everything you need to know about the rigours of software ownership?

Nope. It would be a horribly long chapter if it was, and it's long enough already.

These are my edited highlights at best and very much a personal perspective. I don't doubt for a moment that I could keep on writing, and if you were to ask many of my colleagues and counterparts, they'd have just as much to say from their perspective and a raft of subjects to include that I've neither touched on nor thought much about.

Still, these are the limitations of writing and there's plenty here to get you started.

And besides, as my policeman father used to tell me, a driving instructor only teaches you how to make a vehicle go forwards, backwards and around corners in a relatively safe fashion so that you're ready to take a test. Learning to drive is what you do once you've passed.

Top SaaS tip: Before you go any further, ask yourself why you're here.

CHAPTER 8

PURPOSE

I finished the previous chapter with a somewhat cryptic top tip suggesting that you ask yourself why you're here. You may find that to be a somewhat unusual question for a man such as myself, who's steeped in a world of logic, science and rationality. You might even think it a little bit of woo-woo, pop psychology or new-age nonsense.

However, you'd be wrong. There is method in my apparent madness.

At various points throughout this book, I've referred to a link between technology and our emotional selves. I've told you that the development of software is an exercise in empathy, and that the better we know and understand our customers' humanity and drivers, the more likely it is that we'll produce a tool that satisfies their needs. And I've explained that when people choose to buy something, they're simply rationalising their emotional decisions.

If that's so, I might also suggest that your decision to make some software and to get into the SaaS world is also some emotional mutton dressed as a lamb. You may think it's a rational decision, but is it really?

So, I'll ask again, why are you here?

WHY?

I was asked the same question on 9 June 2018 at an invitational event in a hotel on the mid north coast of New South Wales and it stopped me in my tracks. I was there, at that location, because I'd been invited to be there, but that wasn't the question they were asking.

They wanted to know why I'd joined Dent Global's Key Person of Influence program; why I'd left a perfectly good job; why I'd decided to become a consultant; why I'd decided to change my status quo.

I thought about it for a moment and said that I wanted to see what happened next, how it was all going to work out and what the future had in store for me. After all, this was less than a year after my epiphany and the realisation that all that had gone before was no longer the right path for me, so I really had no idea what lay ahead, and to say I was a little anxious would be somewhat of an understatement.

But that was then, and my journey of the last four years has taught me much. If you'd asked me the same question a couple of years ago, I'd have told you confidently and clearly that I now understand that I exist at the intersection of technology and education, and that I do what I do because I want to share my knowledge with as many people as I can to help them create an exceptional digital future.

Considering where I started, such an organised articulation of what motivated me and what I was hoping to achieve was beyond my wildest fantasies.

But that's not what I'd say today, because if one is going to dream of great things one might as well dream big, and by big, I mean huge in the world-changingly MASSIVE sense.

And why not? I don't suppose I have anything better to do.

MY NEW PURPOSE

The room full of entrepreneurs engaging in conscious capitalism, the environment, social purpose and the UN Global Goals in chapter one, and the just mentioned invitational event were one and the same, and for me it was life changing. Four and a half years on, and I once more find myself wondering what will happen next. This time though, I have a new purpose. I know what I want to do, and I know the difference I want to make.

I still exist at the intersection of technology and education, and I still want to share my knowledge, but previously I wanted to make a living and help a few people live a more profitable existence. Today I have far loftier ideals.

Today I want to help you change your life as you embark or continue on your SaaS journey, and in return, I'd like you to change the lives of some people as well. But not just a few, or even a few thousand.

Hundreds of thousands.

Maybe even *millions*.

I'd like you to help me, and this industry that I love, make purposeful action an everyday activity for millions of technology users around the world.

If doing that can earn me an income as well, I'll be a very happy man indeed.

HOW?

Back in chapter one, I wrote, 'Billions of people are exposed to technology every day, whether at work, shopping, travelling, playing or whatever. And where others see scale, I see opportunity. A massive opportunity to unite humanity and to leverage technology and our connection to make the world a better place.'

Now that we've enjoyed each other's company for a few hours, it's time for me to explain myself a little more, and for once I'm going to gush a little about technology. I promise it will be brief though.

Software is an enabler

Software is the thread that connects us all. It sits at the centre of our lives, quietly going about its business, and we barely pay it a moment's notice any more. We simply pick up our devices and tap away at the screen, checking messages, reading the news and responding to notifications for our little endorphin hits like lab rats tapping away at a feeder bar in the hope of the next reward. We manage our banking, play games, apply for jobs and pay for our groceries using a single device that we keep in our pockets and take everywhere.

Our technology enables our achievement of the extraordinary. If the billions of people connected to each other via the internet isn't enough for you, the James Webb space telescope, a device so unbelievably complex and perfect, has been launched into space and is now telling us about events billions of years ago. And then there's the CERN Large Hadron Collider teaching us about the fundamental building blocks that make up our world.

This is what we can do with technology when we are organised, when we work together as a team to target an outcome. It's rare that I use the word 'awesome', but if you're not profoundly awestruck by what humans have achieved with mastery of this technological world, you're what I'd refer to as a tough [preferred expletive] crowd.

And yet, there is so much more we can do, particularly for ourselves and our fellow humans.

We're lucky

When I consider my circumstances, I have to admit that I've won the human lottery. And if you're reading this, it's highly likely that you have too. You doubtless have food, shelter, warmth, you're probably living in a comparatively rich country and nothing has tried to turn you into lunch.

I bet, like me, you go out for dinner every now and then, or go shopping at the mall and buy clothes made in far-off nations. If you're the relatively conscientious sort, you might leave a tip for the restaurant team, or check the store to make sure they're not engaged in slavery or questionable supply chain activities.

I'm sure you pay for a few online services for a small monthly fee too, or perhaps you use remote workers who deliver their services for a fraction of the price because they live in relative poverty.

I do too.

How much attention do you pay to them?

Ten measly dollars

I posted a job for some artwork on a site once and a young Filipino guy offered to do the work for $100 or so. I liked his portfolio, so I accepted and then I did something that, to this day, I still feel a little uncomfortable about.

I haggled over the price to save $10.

Seriously!

And at the time I felt like I'd won.

Hindsight however is a cruel mistress. It happened a few days before my trip to that hotel on the mid north coast of New South Wales, and on the way I found myself feeling rather guilty and wondering why I'd done it. I questioned my motivation for asserting my dominance, for trying to get one over on someone with far greater needs than me. I even thought if I'd been charged a little extra, I wouldn't have minded.

It was the first time I'd ever thought that, and while I didn't know it then, I'd just had the idea that today defines the future I'd like to build.

The power of small

Businesses like B1G1 and Pledge1Percent help entrepreneurs and organisations give to the community and charitable causes through micro donations, some as small as one US cent. These are without doubt entirely admirable, and they should be lauded, but I always thought it odd that the business should be the one doing the good on behalf of its customers.

Then there are others like GoodCompany in Australia. It helps enterprises embed giving, providing ways for the team to donate regularly and taking a dollar-for-dollar contribution from the employer. Again, utterly fabulous. Yet once more I find it odd that it's the business effectively doing most of the hard yards.

But it was my association with WiseTech Global that began to bring my thinking into focus.

WiseTech's CargoWise platform facilitates the movement of billions of parcels and packages around the planet, simplifying supply chain management, customs and much more for thousands of businesses. Its customers include the likes of DHL who deliver over 1.5 billion parcels every year, and FedEx who deliver over 3 billion. And then there's their latest deal with an up-and-coming business called UPS, and they deliver over 6 billion.

I remember thinking that all of that was going to keep a lot of trains, planes, ships and automobiles on the move and create huge quantities of CO_2, plastic waste and pollution, and we should all, quite rightly, expect those organisations to do something to mitigate the damage they're causing.

And then it hit me!

Why should we expect a handful of businesses to clean up what hundreds of thousands of us asked them to deliver? When we get on a plane, we pay an additional green levy. Why shouldn't DHL et al do the same?

Why shouldn't UPS charge a couple of cents extra? A tiny contribution that no one would ever notice or complain about that could be used to offset the damage, perhaps to plant trees or remove plastic from the oceans.

And who better to facilitate such activities than a software company that supplies some of the platforms used by these behemoths.

> **Top SaaS tip: If not you, then who? If not now, then when?**

The power of scale

If such an idea would make logical sense for the logistics industry, there seems to be no reason why it wouldn't apply to all industries. Surely there must be numerous vendors who could offer something similar for their market.

And of course, there are. There are tens of thousands, and they all have the perfect opportunity.

If you're the CEO of a SaaS business, you have a community and many of them are willing to listen. Better still, you're the leader. You control the room, and you have the mic. You have an opportunity to speak to the masses, so all you need to do is work out what you want to say.

So why not tell the many retail customers who pay $10 every month for your service that you're going to add 10¢ extra to be used for a good purpose? That's an extra $1.20 each per year and if you have 10,000 customers, a princely sum of $12,000 to spend on something purpose-led.

Did you know that just one US cent can buy clean drinking water for one person for a day, or seeds to be planted for food?

But what if you're Zoom, with 300,000,000 calls every day? Well, many of those are free users, but there are many businesses and entrepreneurs who pay, and I'm sure just one cent extra per call would result in a very large pile of cash just waiting to be used to create an impact.

And what about all that paid advertising we see everywhere? Imagine if Google and Facebook asked for just a few cents extra for every paid ad?

Then there's your local supermarket. What if they took a few cents extra for every basket going through the checkouts? Every customer with a loyalty card automatically doing their bit to spread the wealth.

One cent extra on every ride with Uber?

Or every app downloaded from the App Store or Google Play?

This is the power of scale.

SCALE, SCALE, SCALE, SCALE … ENORMOUS GREAT SCALE!

The power of software

At the centre of all of these opportunities lies software, and in practical terms, it would require very little work to implement the necessary functionality. After all, it's just a little extra money on every payment. All it would require is an option for the customer to opt in or opt out if they were so inclined, something you could of course bake in from the very beginning as you're putting together your SaaS venture.

This is the power of software. While artificial intelligence and our many other advances offer so much for tomorrow, the tools we have today are still extraordinarily powerful, and what they excel at is repeating the same process over and over again at massive scale.

As I say, if you're looking at the technology, you're missing the point. We have the tools available, what we need is to organise the masses and make giving so simple they can't help but do it.

YOUR NEW PURPOSE

As I hope I've explained, those of us at the sharp end of the ubiquitous SaaS and software world have an extraordinary opportunity to do something truly world changing.

There are of course many occasions when just because we can we most definitely shouldn't, like abusing a position of trust and power, parking on the train tracks or eating yellow snow. But in this particular case, I'm of the opinion that if we can, we absolutely should. In fact, I see no good reason not to.

Top SaaS tip: With great power comes great opportunity.

So, I'll ask you again.

Why are you here?

If you're driven by money and you fancy being the next Zuckerberg, and perhaps spending the evening doing cash angels in a pit full of $50 bills, I say go for it. It's a perfectly reasonable desire and I sincerely wish you well.

You can always do some good once you get rich.

If you're driven by a desire to use your knowledge, help your people solve their problems, and maybe make a few, or more, dollars along the way, I say go for that too. It's where a great many SaaS leaders start.

You too can always do some good once you have a little cash to spare.

But, if you're driven to help your people, to make a difference, to help those less fortunate than yourself, give someone a better life, right a wrong, put a smile on someone's face, feed the hungry, clothe the cold, house the homeless or whatever good things you can do, why not make helping people the purpose of your business?

You can do some good every day, from the moment you start planning your business.

So why not make it the very reason you're here?

No purpose and purpose

Last century, if you'd asked the typical CEO what the purpose of their business was, they'd have likely told you either a business goal, such as being the biggest widget maker in the country, or the usual of making the best possible return for the shareholders.

A very self-centred purpose if ever there was one.

As we headed towards the new millennium, purpose statements started to become fashionable, and they're still very much in vogue. Woolworths for example currently says this.

> *The world is constantly changing and Woolworths Group has evolved, too. With a connected and unified purpose at its heart, our new Group identity showcases the impact Woolworths Group makes when we unite with a collective and genuine commitment to create a better tomorrow.*

That's good to know. I have no idea what it means though.

It's all very 'meh' if you ask me.

So what about their major competitor, Coles?

Their purpose is to 'sustainably help all Australians lead healthier, happier lives.'

Now that's a step in the right direction.

They go on to say:

> *This is why we exist. We have an important role to play to sustainably help all Australians. From food waste to a sustainable food chain, we want to be sure we're here for another century, creating jobs, supporting our suppliers and making a positive difference in our local communities.*

Hmm …

That's pretty good. I think I'm about to change supermarket.

Purpose-led

And then there's apparel vendor Patagonia:

> *We're in business to save our home planet.*

Now that's what I call a purpose.

While I've been writing this book, Patagonia, after nearly 50 years in private hands, has changed the business world for ever. Rather than 'going public', it's 'going purpose'. Below is a direct quote from the website by founder Yvon Chouinard.

> *Instead of extracting value from nature and transforming it into wealth for investors, we'll use the wealth Patagonia creates to protect the source of all wealth.*
>
> *100% of the company's voting stock transfers to the Patagonia Purpose Trust, created to protect the company's values; and 100% of the nonvoting stock had been given to the Holdfast Collective, a non-profit dedicated to fighting the environmental crisis and defending nature. The funding will come from Patagonia: Each year, the money we make after reinvesting in the business will be distributed as a dividend to help fight the crisis.*

Rather than risk his life's work at the hands of a bunch of corporate money men and women, Yvon has protected his investment. The title of the page is 'Earth is now our only shareholder'.

Patagonia is a purpose-led organisation. Its purpose defines what it does, how it works, how it sources materials, what it does with the roughly $100 million it makes in profit and so much more. It is an exemplar, and I strongly recommend you find out more about them. Yvon Chouinard's story is utterly inspirational.

Here's the kicker

Whatever your motivations for getting into the SaaS world, I strongly recommend that you make a concerted effort to create a purpose-led business.

I don't say that because it's the right thing to do, though it clearly is.

I don't say it because I want you to help address child poverty, or to feed the starving, though I do.

I don't say it because I want you to help save the planet, which my daughter and, I hope, grandchildren will greatly appreciate.

I say it for two specific purposes.

The first is this.

It is *my* new purpose to make purposeful action an everyday activity for millions of technology users around the world, and I can't do that on my own.

The second might surprise you.

I want you to create a purpose-led business because, statistically, it will make you more money!

Yes, you read that right.

MONEY!

This is nothing to do with being a good person, getting to heaven or any of that other goody-two-shoes nonsense. This is just me giving you a little sound professional advice.

Doing good in the 2020s quite simply improves the bottom line and purpose-led businesses outperform their counterparts.

And by outperform, I mean they kick their pathetic, pitiful, purposeless arse.

Damn! I love an alliteration.

By the numbers

In 2018, management consultants Development Dimensions International reported that businesses with no purpose statement underperformed the market by 42%. Those with a purpose statement only performed roughly at the mean.

PURPOSE-LED businesses outperformed the market by a staggering 42%.

Brand value

According to Forbes, just about every brand health measure was far superior for PURPOSE-LED businesses.

One survey found that 66% of consumers would drop their usual brand in favour of another from a purpose-driven company. And if we're talking about millennials, those in their mid-twenties to early forties, the figure rises to 91%.

If you think that's stunning, wait until you see what the next generation has in store for you. Gen Z consumers are 85% more likely to trust a brand, 84% more likely to buy their products, and 82% more likely to recommend that brand to friends and family if it's PURPOSE-LED.

The *Wall Street Journal* found that nearly 60% of Americans would avoid a brand if it had a negative position on societal issues, and that was up nearly a quarter on the year before. That figure was mirrored in an Edelman survey which found that 64% of people worldwide shared that same sentiment.

Nielsen found that roughly two-thirds of people would pay more for something if the brand were committed to making a positive social impact.

You paying attention yet?

Accenture asked 30,000 consumers what they thought, and over 60% said they wanted companies to take a stand on relevant issues such as sustainability, transparency and fair work practices. In 2020 Deloitte found that 'authentic purpose is now as important as digital to the next generation of customers.' In 2019, New Paradigm Strategy Group & Fortune found that nearly two-thirds of adults in the US thought a business's 'primary purpose' should be 'making the world a better place'.

Should I go on?

You know I'm going to.

Employers and employees

According to LinkedIn, 74% of its users put a high value on a job with a sense of purpose.

In 2019, Cone/Porter Novelli reported that over 80% of Gen Z Americans take a company's purpose into consideration when choosing an employer. Better Up told us in 2018 that over 90% of employees would swap some of their lifetime earnings if it meant a greater meaning at work. Danone/YouGov found in 2018 that over 50% would consider leaving a job if their employer's values and purpose didn't align with their own.

As far back as 2014, the LMU Center for Economic Studies found that employees who feel they're working towards a good cause can increase their productivity by as much as 30%. In 2018, Mercer spoke with 7500 employees and found that the best performers are three times more likely to take a job with a business with a strong sense of purpose.

A bandwagon worth joining

I'm pretty sure you're getting the gist of this now, and if you're not I'll hammer you with one last purpose-related statistic, and this time it's nothing to do with technology because as you now know …

In 2019, a public health and retirement study of nearly 7000 US citizens aged over 50 found that there is a strong correlation between having a sense of purpose in life and physical and mental wellbeing. Incredibly, those with the lowest sense of purpose had a mortality rate over twice as high.

Finding a purpose, it seems, is very much part of the human condition. It's something inherent in our nature. The more purpose we find in our lives, the happier we are and the healthier we are.

Perhaps then, by becoming a purpose-led business and delivering a platform that helps make the world a better place, you'll not only serve the needs of those who benefit from the social good that you do, you might just help a few of your customers find a sense of purpose too.

Now wouldn't that be a thing.

Top SaaS tip: If you want a long and lustrous life, find a purpose worth living for.

EMBEDDING YOUR PURPOSE

Finding ways to generate a little extra from your customers shouldn't really be that much of a problem. As I've already outlined, our regular interactions with technology offer many opportunities. Even those who feel compelled to offer a freemium version can get involved.

Remember my comments from before?

If not, here's a reminder. If you don't want to make a dollar for yourself from it, fair enough. But rather than giving it away, why not ask for a one-off $10 donation to fund charitable impact aligned with your purpose? You might even go as far as matching the amount. That way you'd really show off your purpose-led credentials.

But, saying you're purpose-led is one thing. *Being* it is another. So I'll start with one of these.

Surprise! A cautionary tale

Asking your customers to donate to a worthy cause seems like the right thing to do, but unsurprisingly, not everyone will appreciate your efforts, especially if your implementation leaves a little bit to be desired.

This is why there are people who specialise in helping businesses embed purpose within the organisation. If you just bolt it on in a somewhat haphazard fashion, you're going to run into problems.

Woolworths in Australia found this out the hard way.

In 2021, it added a donation facility to self-service checkouts. When you pay it asks if you'd like to round up to the nearest dollar, with the contribution being sent to a children's charity.

Good stuff, huh?

Well, yes, but there were a few problems, not least of which is that Woolworths has a fairly poor reputation when it comes to the amount of perfectly good food it throws away and not treating farmers overly well. This was typified in 2018 when it and Coles came up with a 'milk levy' to be added to some milk brands to support drought-affected farmers. These were the same farmers who'd had their prices slashed by the supermarkets in the first place.

It also made nearly two billion dollars in profit.

Insult was added to injury when some of the checkouts asked for a donation and gave two choices of 'Yes' and 'Yes, please'.

As I'm sure you can imagine, this went down very well on social media, and it was pointed out that if Woolworths was truly interested in making a difference it could match the amount donated. This would have been a tiny sum of money for them, but huge for the charity.

If only.

It's a lifestyle choice

Being a purpose-led business means that everything you do needs to point towards your stated aim. You can't just say it, write a couple of blog posts and then move on. If you do that, you'll be found out very quickly and the savage hordes that inhabit the many socials will rip you to shreds.

I face the same problem. Having stated here and in my social media content that I'd like to achieve something, I'd appear somewhat dubious if the next business I advise doesn't embed a purpose, or at least look like it's trying to do some good in the world. Happily, I don't think that's going to be a problem.

And you can't just bluff your way through either. The best you'll do is to make it look like you're greenwashing, a term used to describe those businesses that put an environmentally sound spin on their marketing to make it look as though they give a shit. If this ever works at all, it doesn't last for long.

The person in the street is generally rather adept at detecting the sickly-sweet smell of bullshit. You might fool some of the people some of the time, but it's not going to end well.

Pobody's nerfect

While you might aim for glory, there's always an inherent risk that you'll be required to do something that is, or at least appears to be, somewhat antithetical. Most notable for SaaS vendors is the use of the cloud and remote storage. The massive data centres used to feed our online obsession consume vast amounts of power and are seen by many as polluters. This is of course true, but in practical terms, centralisation of systems is far more efficient than having many individual suppliers.

What's perhaps most important is that you don't try to hide from your failings, perceived or otherwise. As any real estate agent will tell you, it's far better to address issues up front than to let a prospective buyer find them out. Patagonia shows us the way once more here. As part of its core values, it highlights that its own business practices, wholly necessary to be able to do the good they do, are in fact part of the problem. However, they're working to improve everything they do and to share what they learn so that others may benefit.

Their aim is simply to cause no unnecessary harm.

Top SaaS tip: You can't build software without creating bugs.

Ten tips for practising what you preach

As ever, implementation is everything, so here's a few tips and ideas to help you start your purpose-led journey.

Define your purpose

This might seem obvious, but you need to be clear about what it is that you want to achieve. Unsurprisingly, this should be something that's aligned with the niche you identified way back at the beginning. After all, if your purpose doesn't resonate well with the humans you're trying you sell to, you're just going to make things hard for yourself.

If you're not sure where to start, consider picking one of the United Nations' 17 Sustainable Development Goals such as gender equality, zero hunger, or peace, justice and strong institutions.

Lead and be led

No matter the size of your organisation, all leaders need to have their eyes on the prize and to lead the team by example. Your purpose should be part of your culture, so while your leadership team is leading the team, your purpose should be leading them.

Involve the team

The more you empower the team to engage with your purpose, the better the results will be. Nothing says we care better than helping your people to get away from their job by giving them a day off so that they can get involved both physically and emotionally.

Evangelists

Just as I recommend evangelists to help with the implementation of a software solution, so too are they a valuable resource when embedding purpose. They help the leadership make appropriate decisions and also encourage the team to become involved.

Celebrate your wins

If you're going to encourage purpose-related activities, you'd be wise to advertise results. Remember, this is as much about culture as it is about actions, so be sure to ring the bell every chance you get. Not only will you continually remind everyone that this is what your organisation is all about, it's a chance for individuals or the whole team to have their name up in lights, and not just internally. Your purpose stories make fantastic marketing copy.

Align your actions

If you're gonna talk the talk, you gotta walk the walk. Whether it's your internal processes, your choice of suppliers and partners, or whatever, you need to continually assess whether a particular facet of your business is doing the right thing and work out what you can do to mitigate the result should it not.

Review and reward

Performance and annual reviews are a perfect opportunity to remind the team of their responsibilities with regards to your purpose and to reward them for their actions. If they've been cutting the mustard, be sure to reward them accordingly. It may be a tiny bit crass, but money is still a great motivator.

It never ends

You may make an initial commitment to a purpose and implement a program of changes to get it up and running, but your work is not done when that program stops. In fact, it is only the end of the beginning, and the beginning of the rest of your life. Like your MVP, it's just the platform on which to build all that follows.

Get tough

If you're going to do this, there's every chance that you're going to need to stand up to the enemy, both without and within. Remember however that purpose-led businesses significantly outperform the market and that many younger workers are increasingly choosing their employer based on whether they are a force for good.

The slings and arrows of outrageous fortune may demand a little pragmatism along the way but stand firm and make sure that a desire for profitability doesn't override your desire to make the world a better place.

Less talk, more action

If you want to practice what you preach, *practice what you preach*. No one's stopping you other than you.

SUMMARY

Whether you're aiming to be purpose-led, striving for sustainability, making an impact, doing good or whatever other way we might find to describe the trend towards philanthropy, giving and generally being a good egg, this is one bandwagon that I strongly recommend you jump on and then cling to for all you're worth.

Giving just 1% of your revenues can transform many lives through the provision of clean drinking water, small infrastructure projects, seeds, food, sanitation, education and so much more. And it's just 1%. If your revenues are $500,000, are you really going to miss $5000?

That's two new laptops for you or about 20,000 days of classroom access for disadvantaged children in Cambodia. All you need to do is sign up with the fine folk at B1G1 and they'll do the rest. Their project requires just 15 US cents for one day's access per child.

If you can get 200 users to pay just $2 extra per month, you can all but double the impact you're making.

See how easy this is?

This is the power of SaaS as it begins to scale.

Being a purpose-led business is good for the team, for recruitment, for your customers, your prospects, your partners, it's good for those who lives are improved thanks to your efforts, and of course it's good for the bottom line.

Quite simply, there is no good reason for not making the focus of your business something that will improve the world just that little bit. I can think of a great many not so good reasons though, and most of them would paint the leadership of a business in a less-than-flattering light. And given that it's increasingly the trend to do the right thing, it's not going be too long before those doing the wrong thing will stand out like the proverbial.

I recall the early days of the internet in the late 1990s when having a website was seen as an expense and there were many business leaders, particularly older ones, who opposed paying for such frivolous nonsense. Retrospect, as I'm wont to say, is a bit of a shit at times.

As ever, the wisdom of the ages has something to teach us. I'm sure you all know you'll catch a lot more flies with honey than you will with vinegar. But, if you're still reading this and your inner curmudgeon is still shaking its head and muttering under its breath that it's not going to give away its hard-earned coin to starving bloody foreigners or woke activists, consider these last few thoughts.

Firstly, this isn't just about saving the whale or undernourished kids in Africa. Charity can start at home. Even here in Australia, there are many causes you can fight for that may even directly improve your world.

Secondly, you don't have to give your money away. You can get your customers to do it. It's just that you'll look a whole heap more authentic if you do as well, and that too is good for business.

Third, no matter how bad your day, you'll always be able to go home safe in the knowledge that while life hasn't gone the way you hoped, you can still enjoy a moment of smug self-satisfaction because your business has achieved its purpose and some people you may never meet will likely go on to live a far better life because they had some clean water and learned to read and write.

And lastly, and just in case I haven't made it abundantly clear, I really couldn't give a shit about how cynical you are about this. I couldn't care one jot if you're the most miserable scumbag on the planet and you're only doing some good because the penny's dropped with a loud thud in the cavernous void you call your brain and you're doing it to improve your own profits. As long as you're using your position of power to help improve the lives of others in need, I will applaud you all day and every day.

I might not like you that much, but I'm pretty sure you'll get over that.

So please, do some good. I promise you, it's worth it on so many levels.

Top SaaS tip: Software + Scale + Purpose = Global Impact

CHAPTER 9

MY END, YOUR BEGINNING

So here we are. That's pretty much it. I'm not going to tell you anything else. There's so much more to say of course but just like a software platform, getting to market is critical, and version one of *Kick Some SaaS* and its audience have a date with destiny. And besides, my good friend Tracy has promised me a cool book launch party, so I really need to wrap things up.

If you're an existing SaaS business owner, I hope we see eye to eye on a range of topics and I hope I've been able to help you improve your game. If we disagree, I'd love to hear about your experiences. There's little I like more in life than being proven wrong because it means I know more tomorrow. If the evidence points to a different conclusion, so be it. I'll update my opinion immediately.

If you're a SaaS wannabe, you'll exist somewhere on a continuum between 'What was I thinking? It's time to get out of Dodge' and 'This is going to be so cool, I can't wait!'

But regardless of who you are and your situation, I hope above all else that you've taken on board the extraordinary opportunity that this world of mine, and I hope ours, has to offer you and yours. We quite literally have the power to change the world.

FOUR PS BECAME FIVE

You've probably worked out by now that the fifth P I mentioned in chapter one is of course Purpose, and that I now need to update all my collateral with my newfound insights. C'est la vie. It's a very nice problem to have.

So here it is, in pride of place with the other four.

- PEOPLE: Connect, customers and community
- PLATFORM: Solution, systems and strategy
- PROMOTION: Campaign, content and conversion
- PARTNERS: Flexibility, fluidity and focus
- PURPOSE: Give, good and get

Purpose tells you that giving will transform your business from that of a simple software vendor to an organisation with a stated goal of doing some good in the world. It permeates the other four pillars, helping you put your many people front and centre, becoming a feature of your platform, changing your stories and how you promote your offering, and enabling new and existing partners to join your cause. And if you give and do some good, there's every chance you'll get your just desserts.

HUMAN-CENTRICITY

And so, with one last thought, I'll sign off. I have a new purpose and there's much to be done. The burgeoning world of software is in its infancy and if it's to grow to best serve the eight billion people on this 'mote of dust suspended in a sunbeam', as Carl Sagan so eloquently described this most beautiful and exceptional home of ours, it's going to need you and me, and many more, to teach it how to be a good global citizen.

So, I wish you well with your SaaS journey, may it take you to places that you never dreamed possible. My own journey continues to astound me almost daily. But it's not the tools I use, the games I play, or the staggering immensity of the technological universe I inhabit that inspires me.

It's you and our eight billion cousins.

For all our imperfections and flaws, it's the beautiful, passionate, dreaming, caring, nurturing, giving, inspiring and loving human family I'm so blessed to be part of.

It's taken my lifetime to understand that, but then, I used to look at the technology.

Top SaaS tip: The responsibility and opportunity are ours, and the time is now.

www.ingramcontent.com/pod-product-compliance
Lightning Source LLC
Chambersburg PA
CBHW071201210326
41597CB00016B/1623